DIESES BUCH GEHÖRT

LINIEN

KREISE

DREIECKE

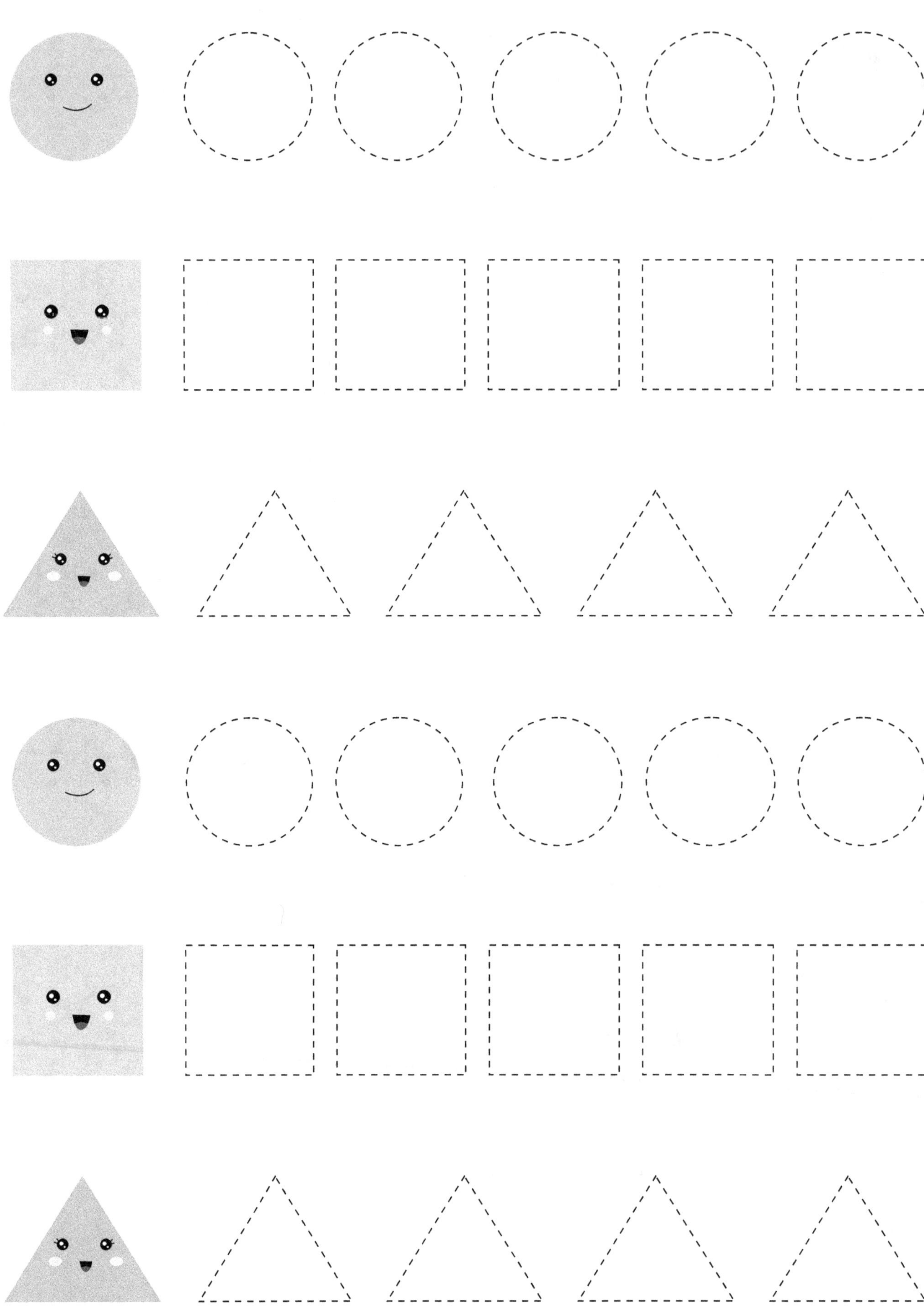

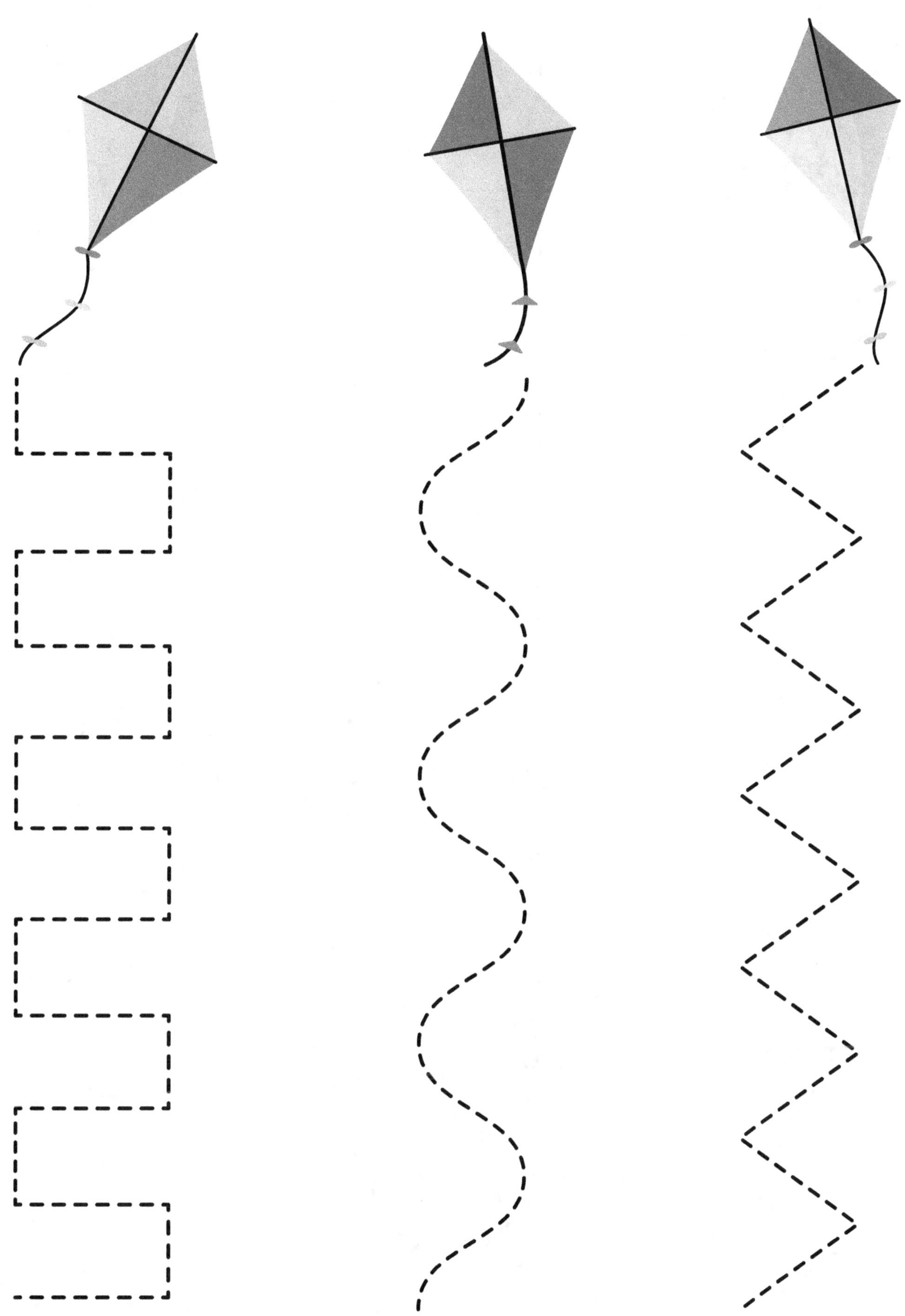

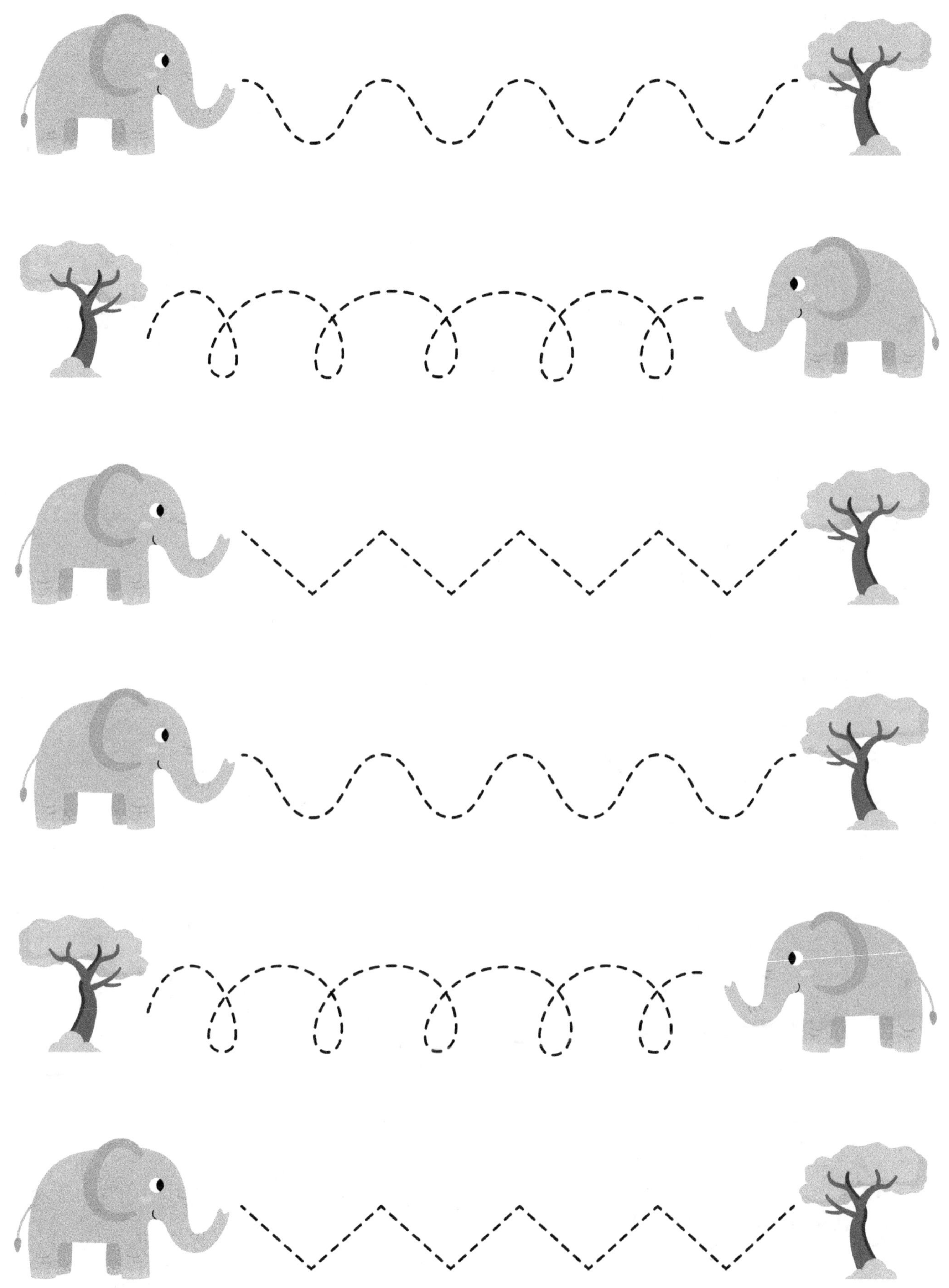

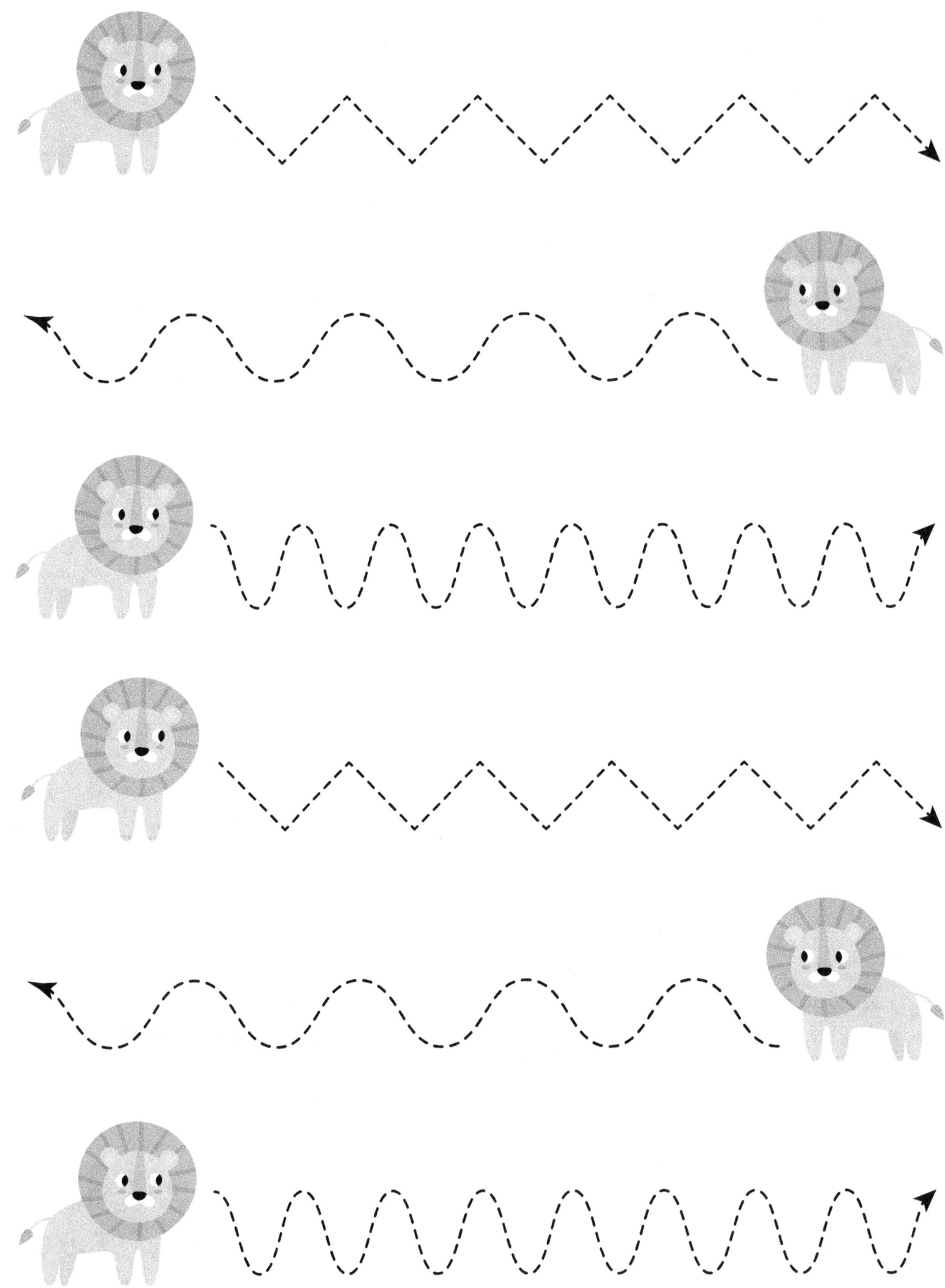

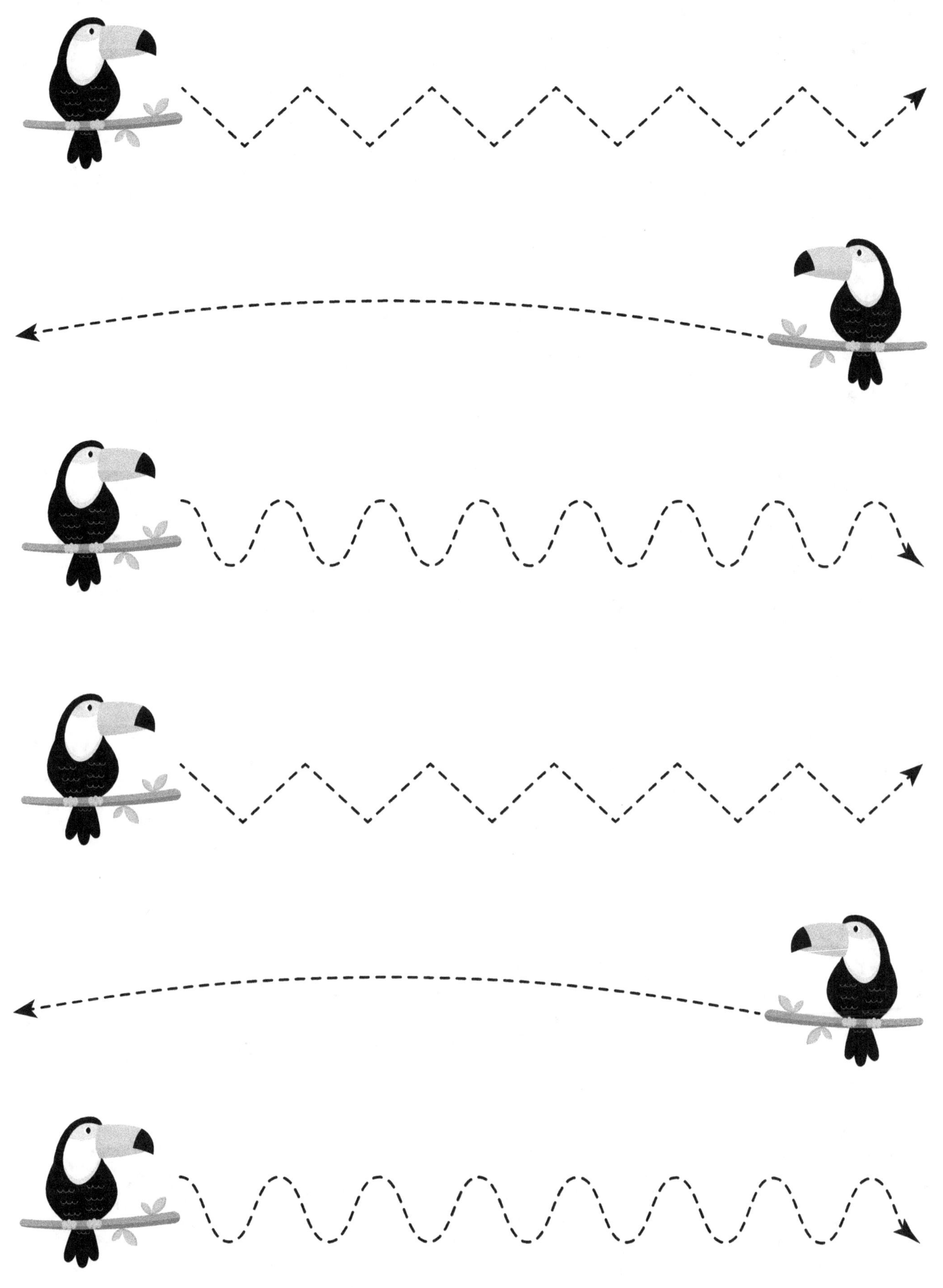

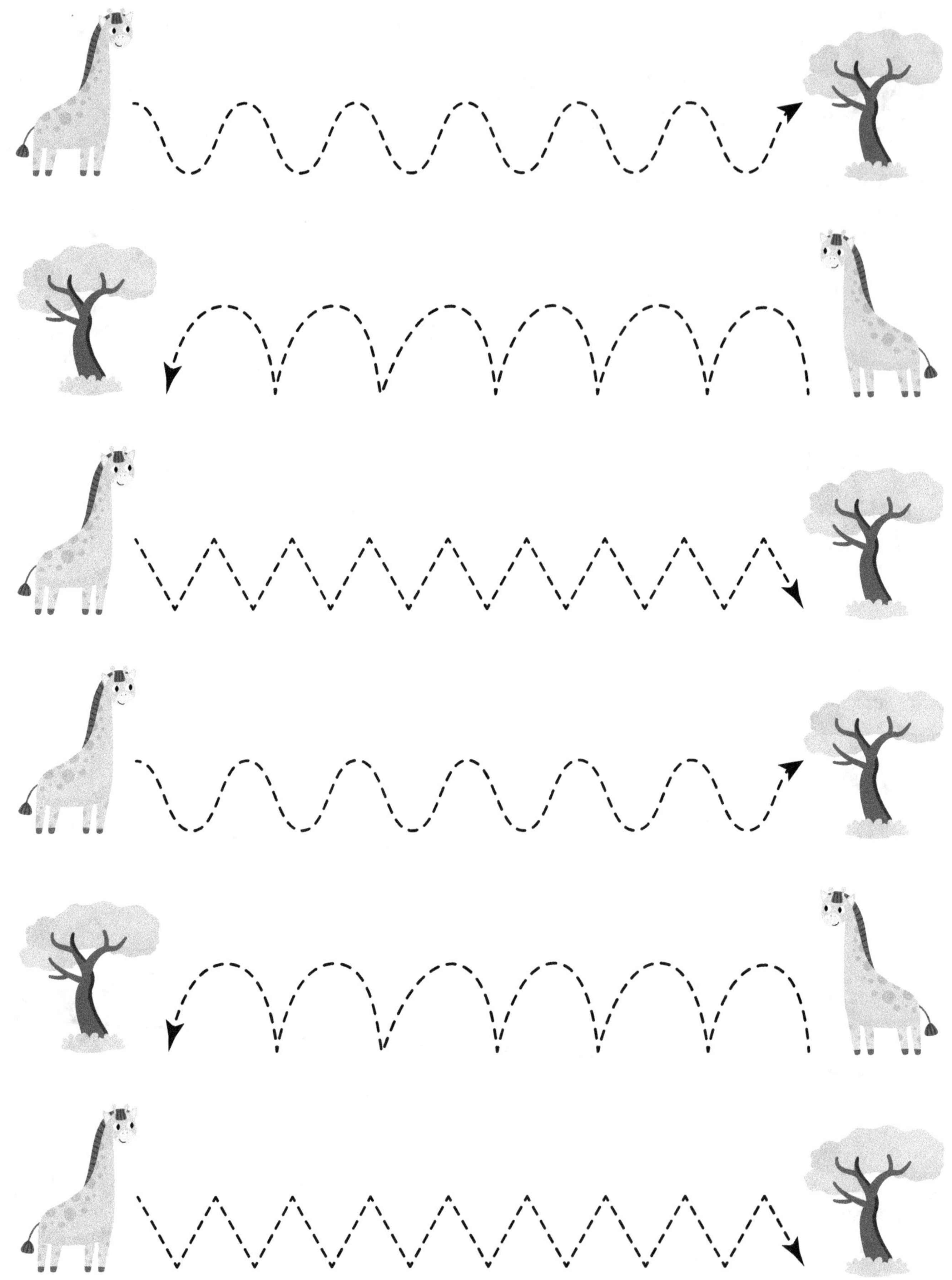

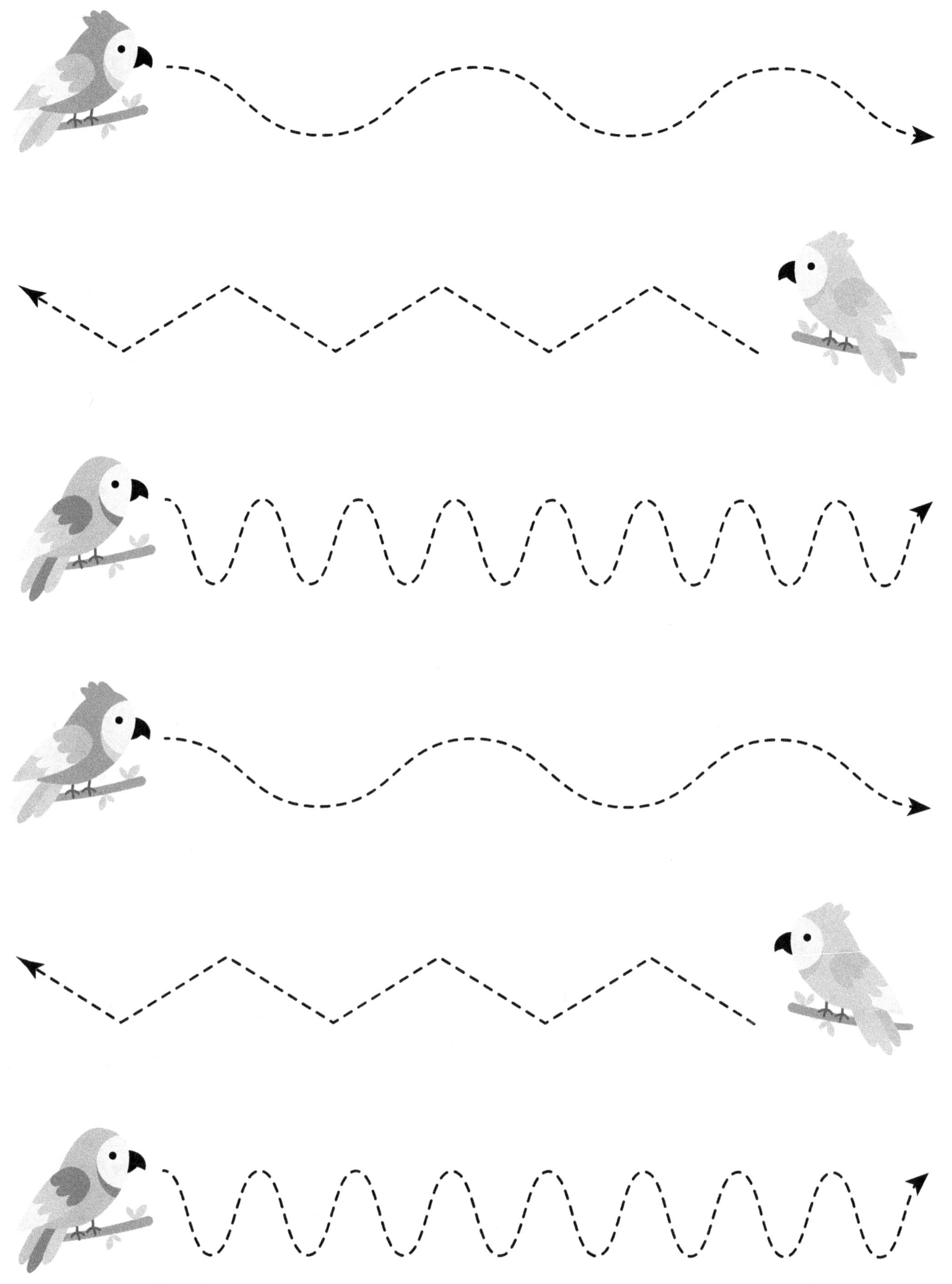

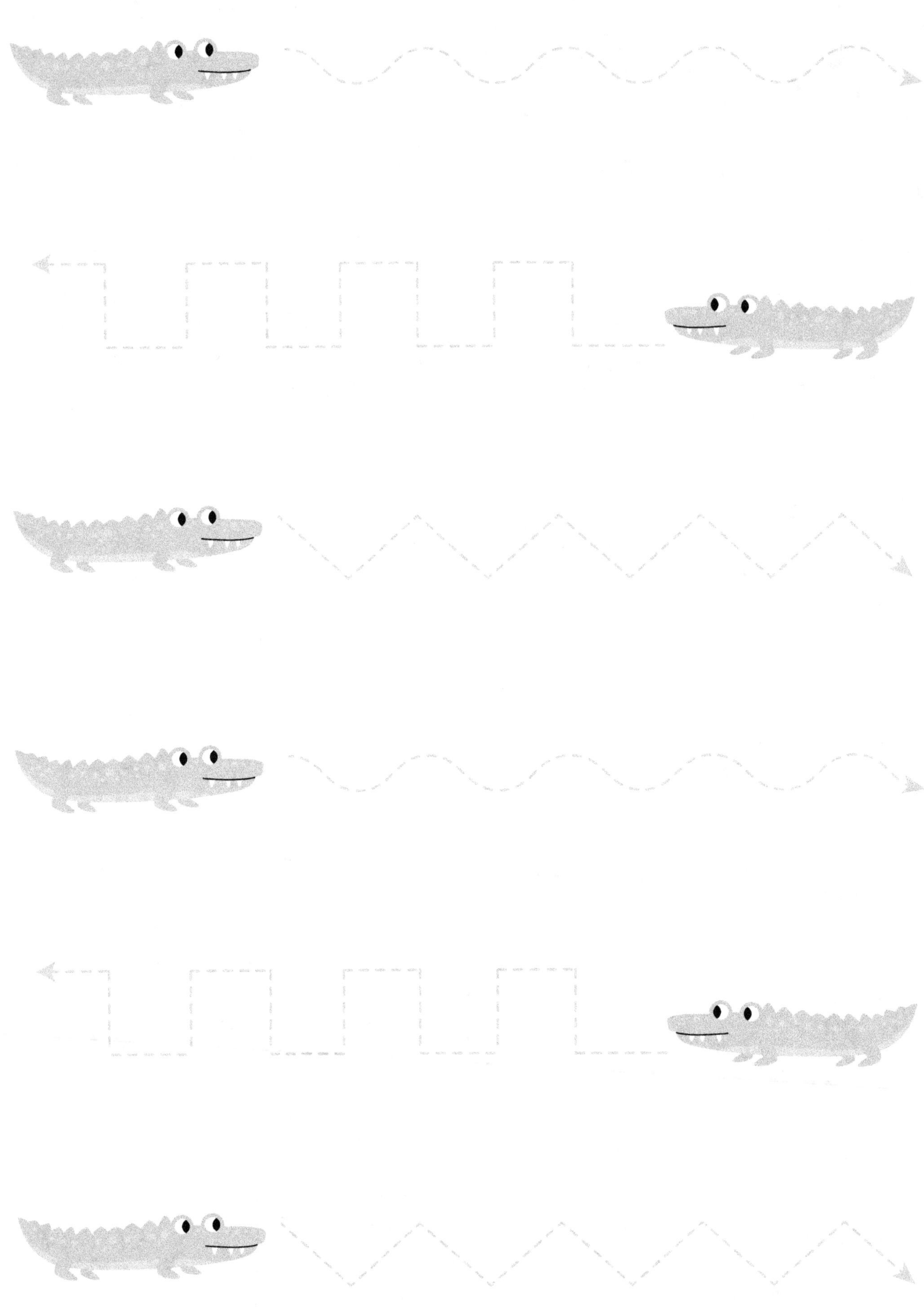

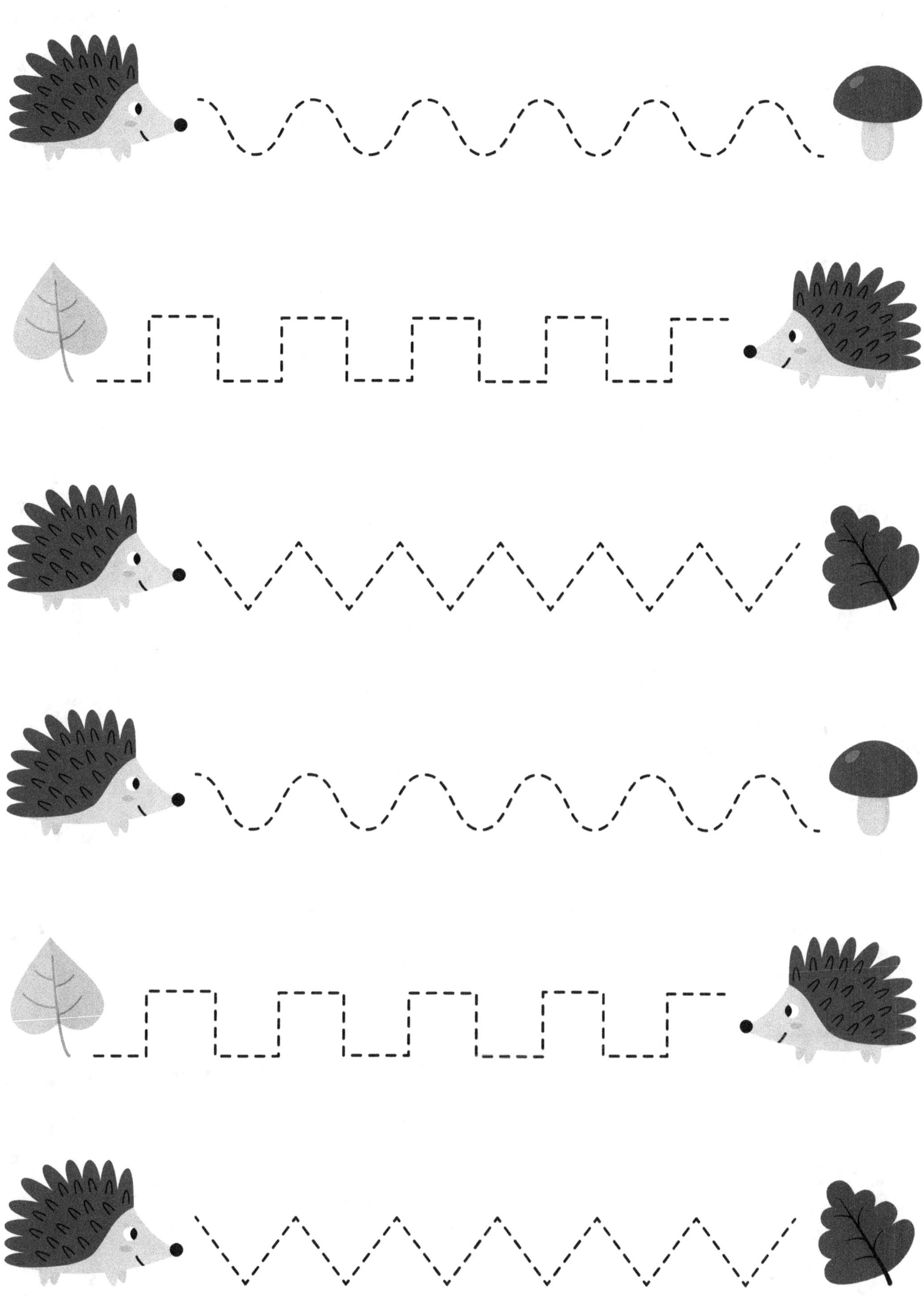

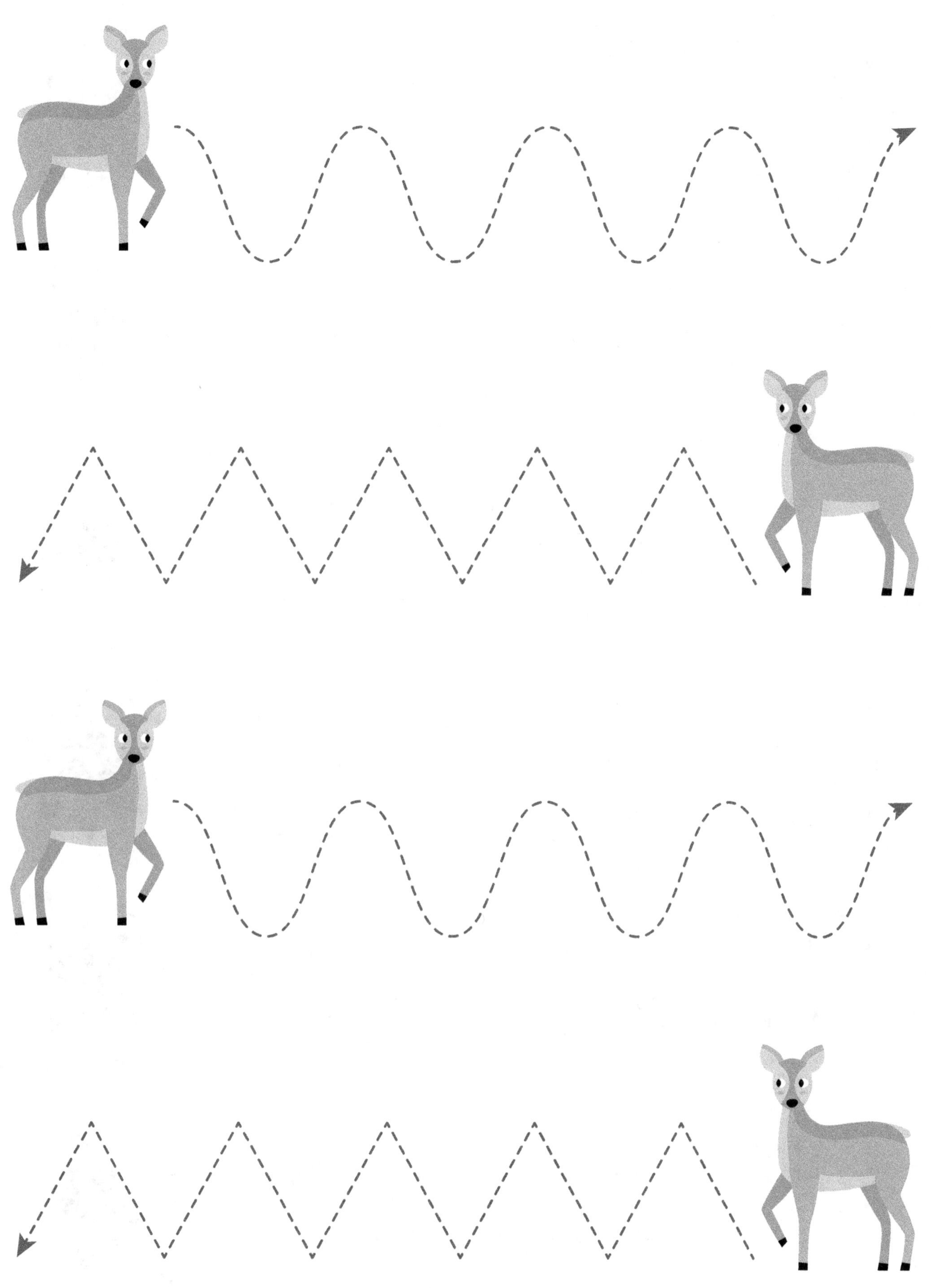

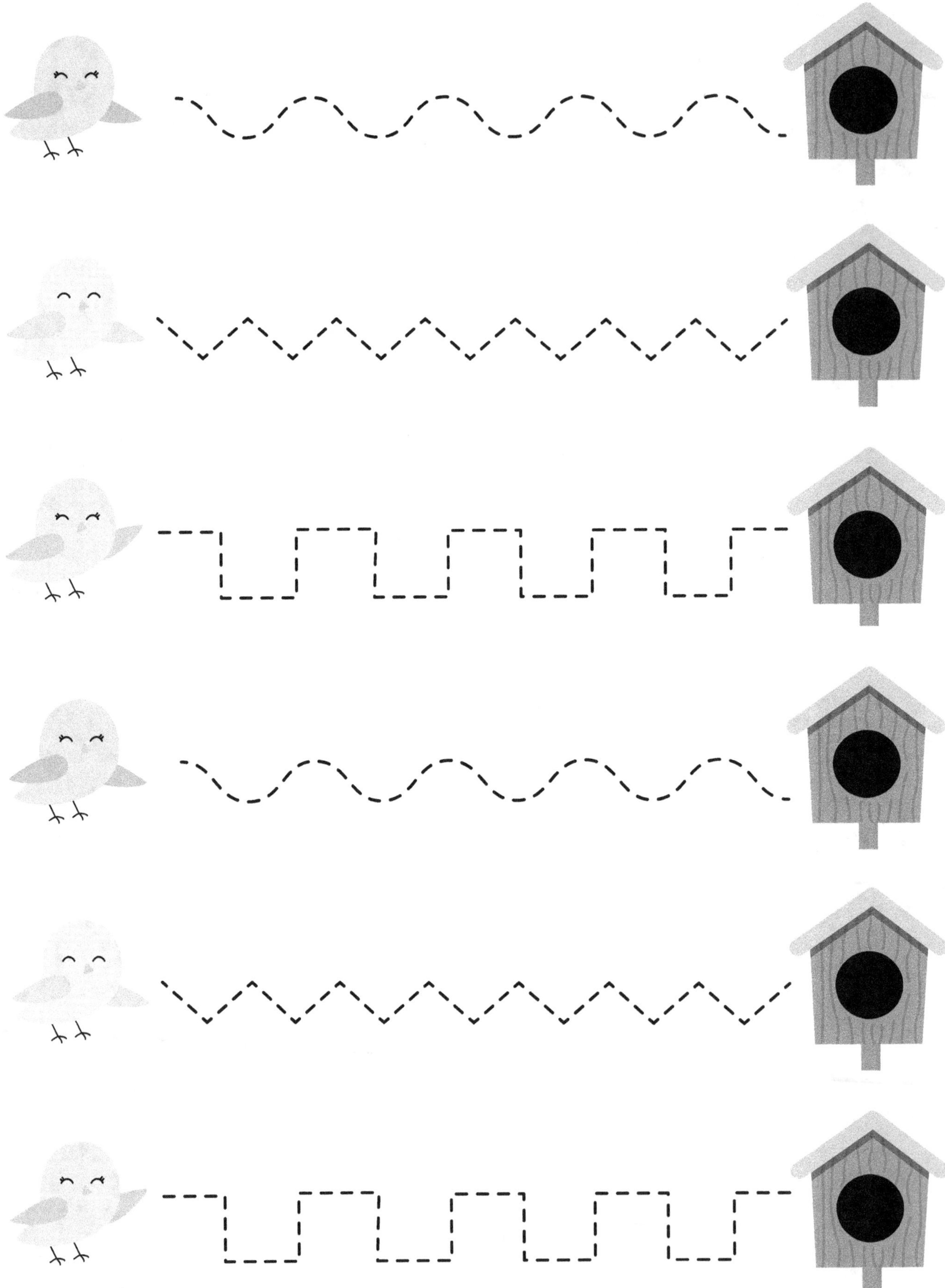

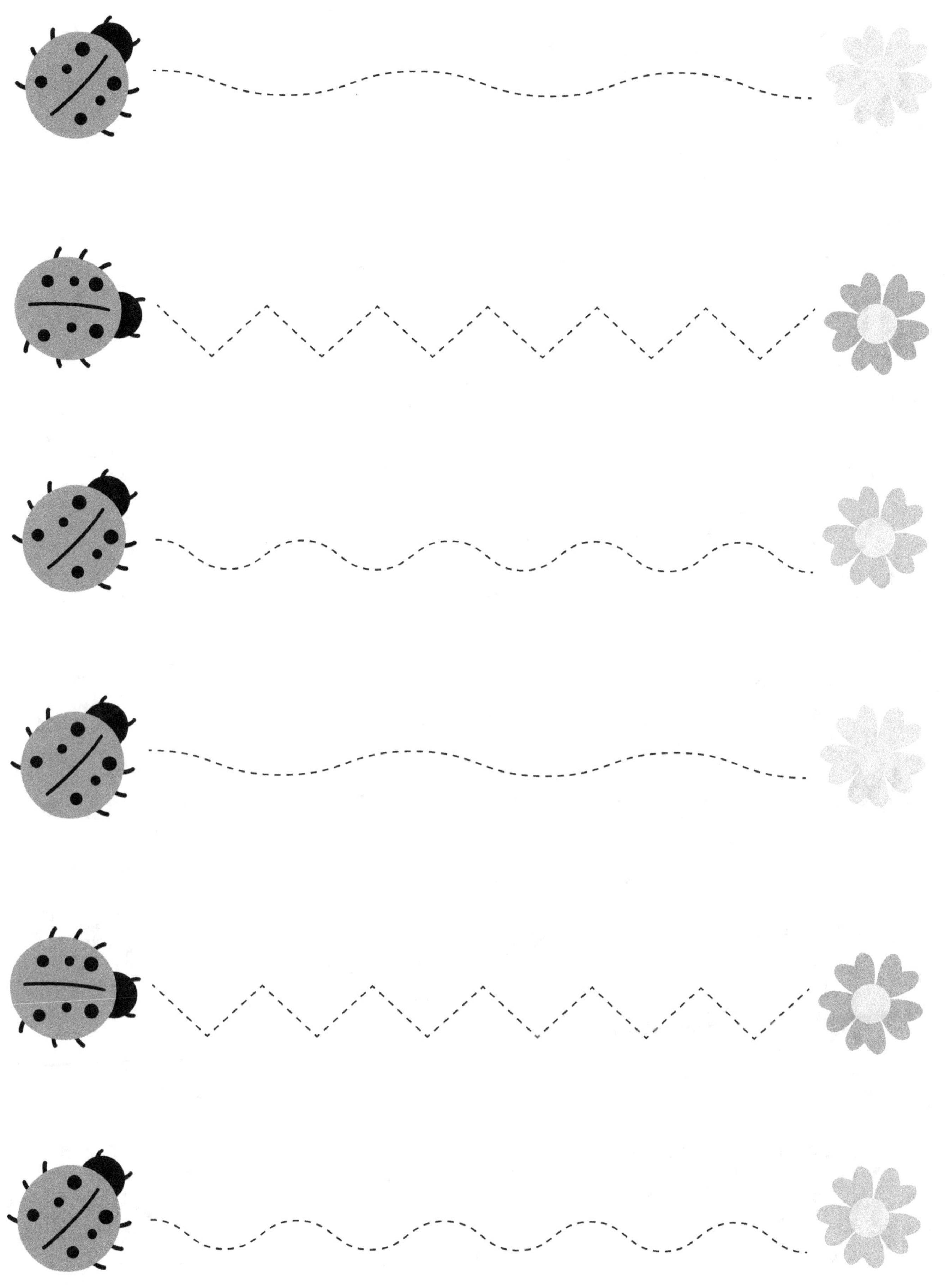

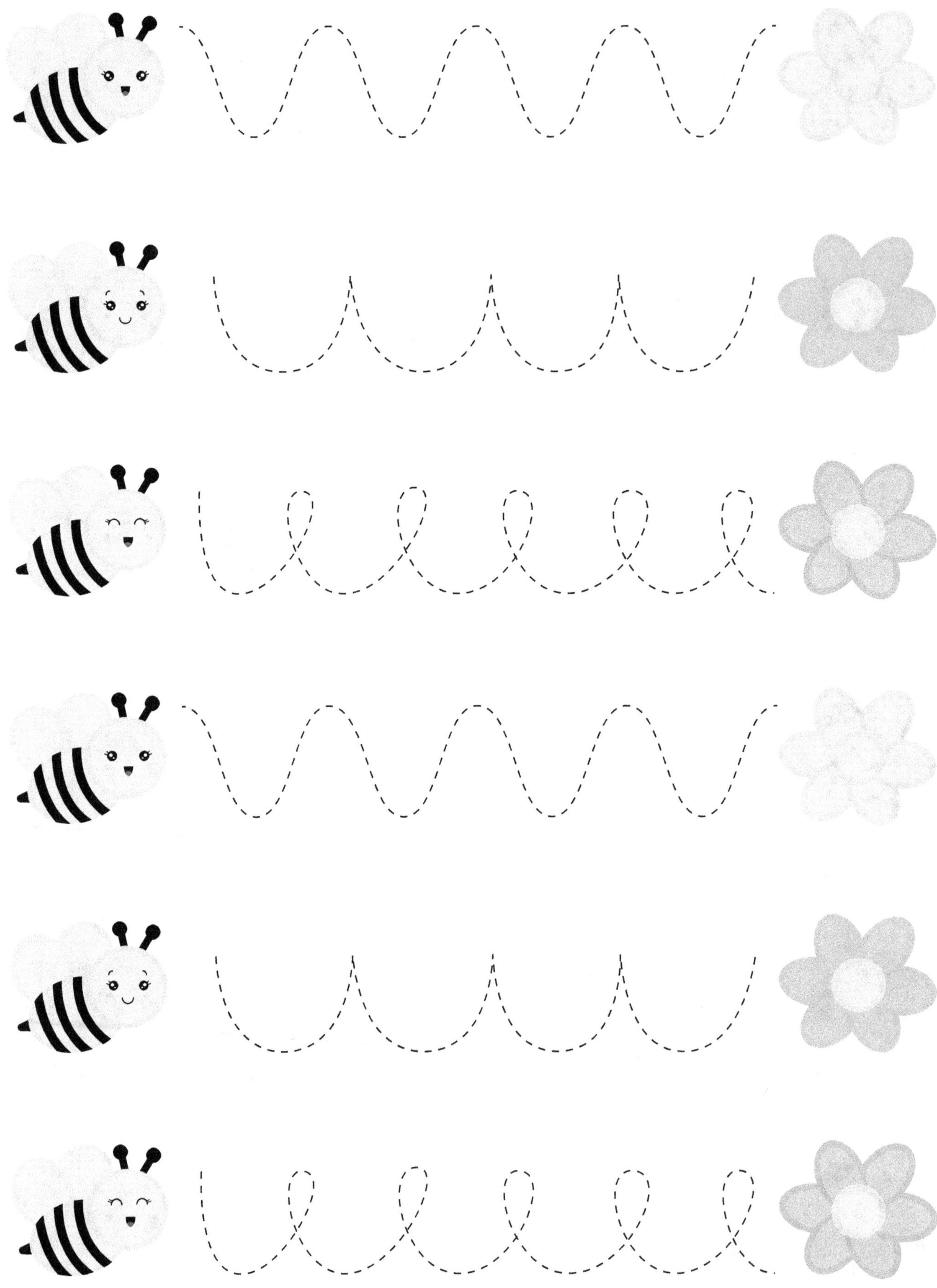

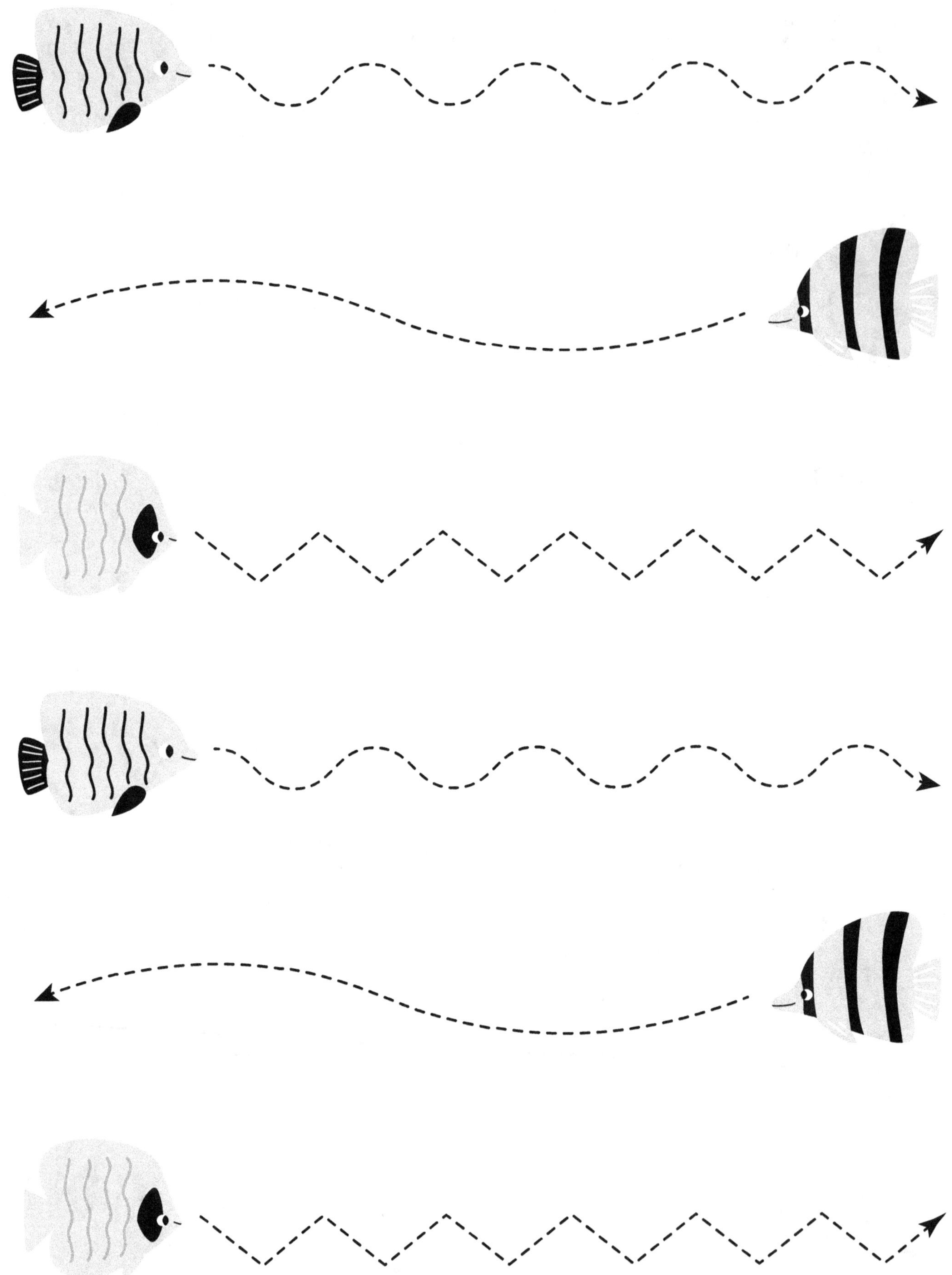

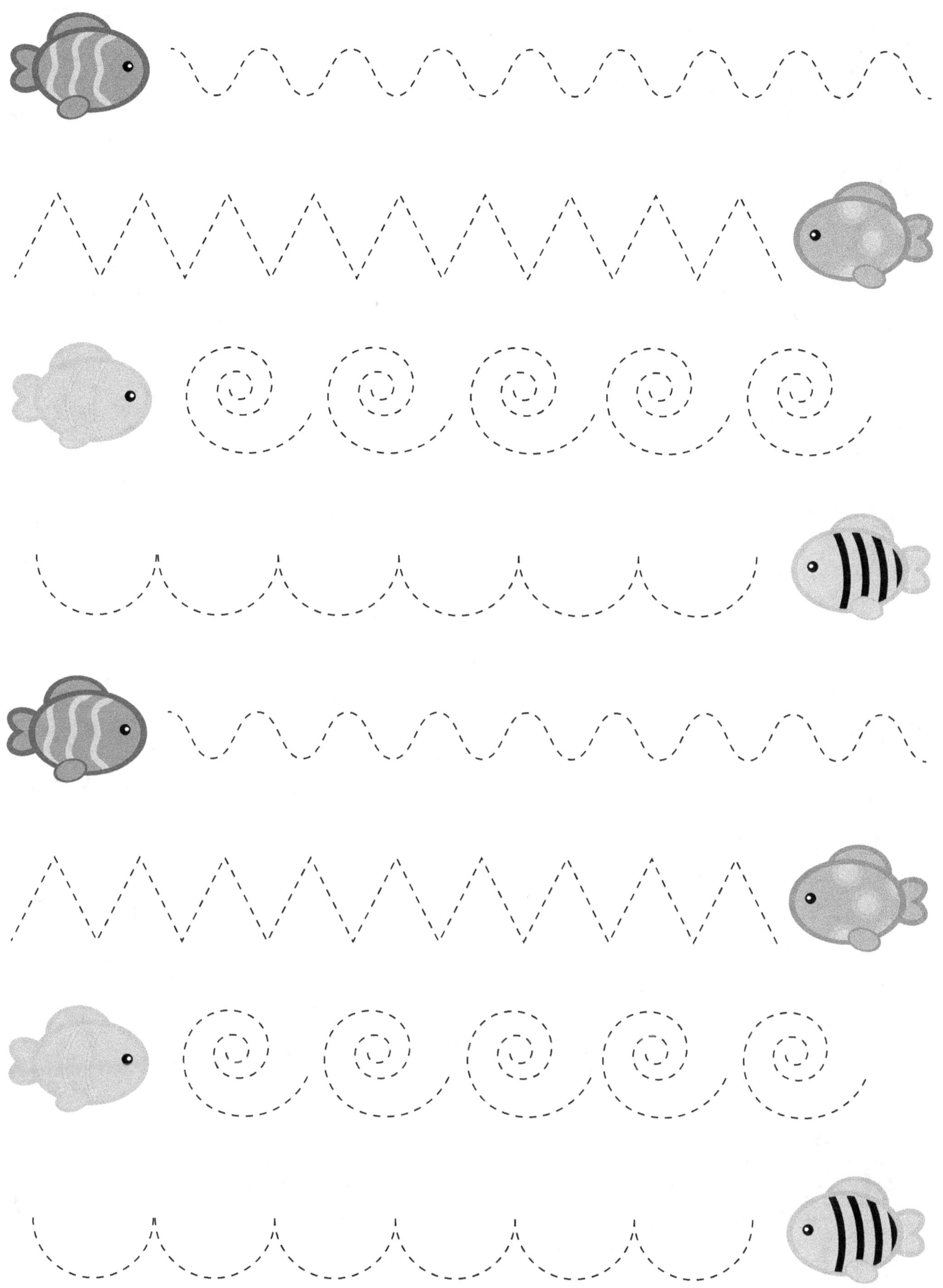

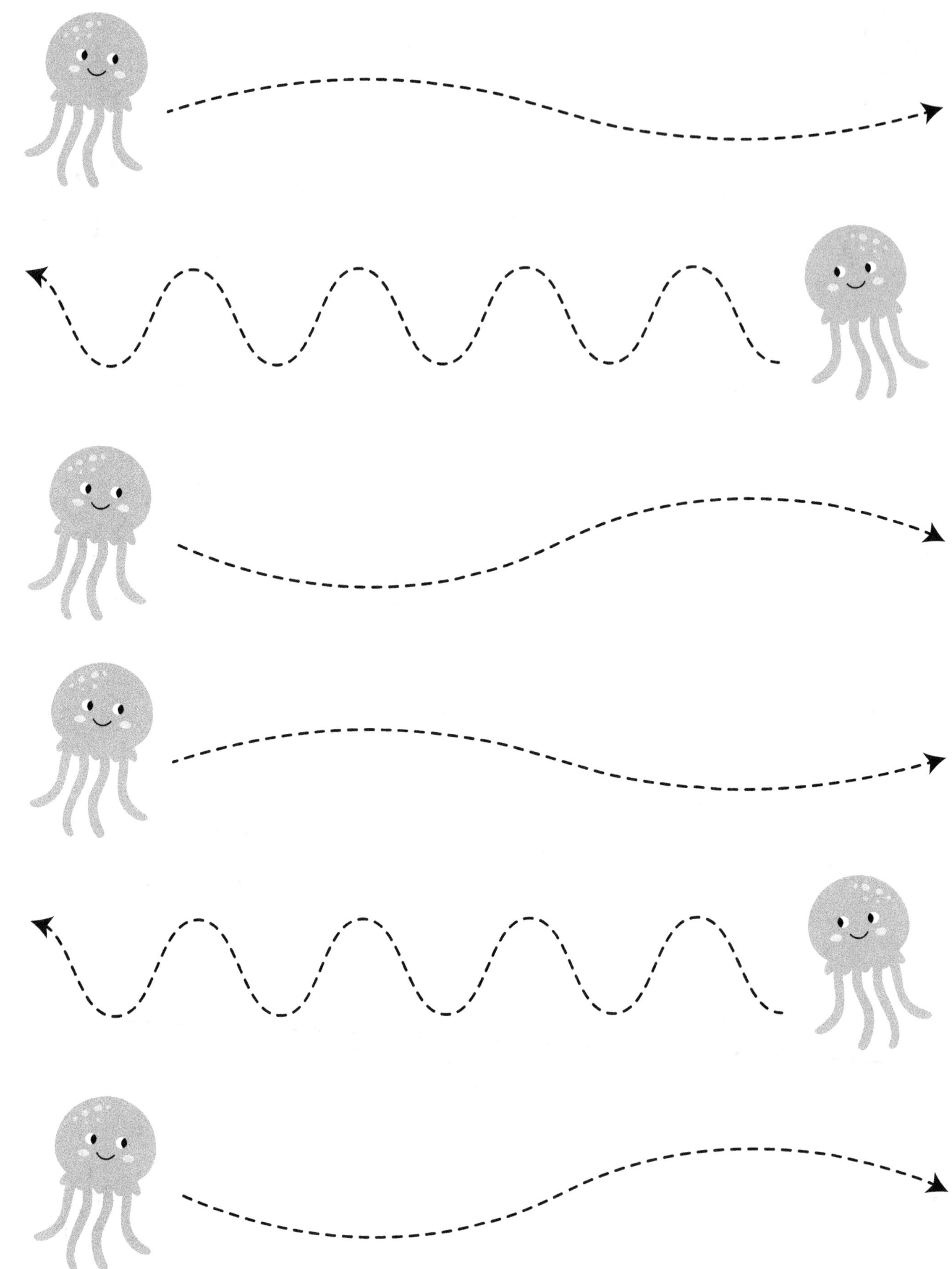

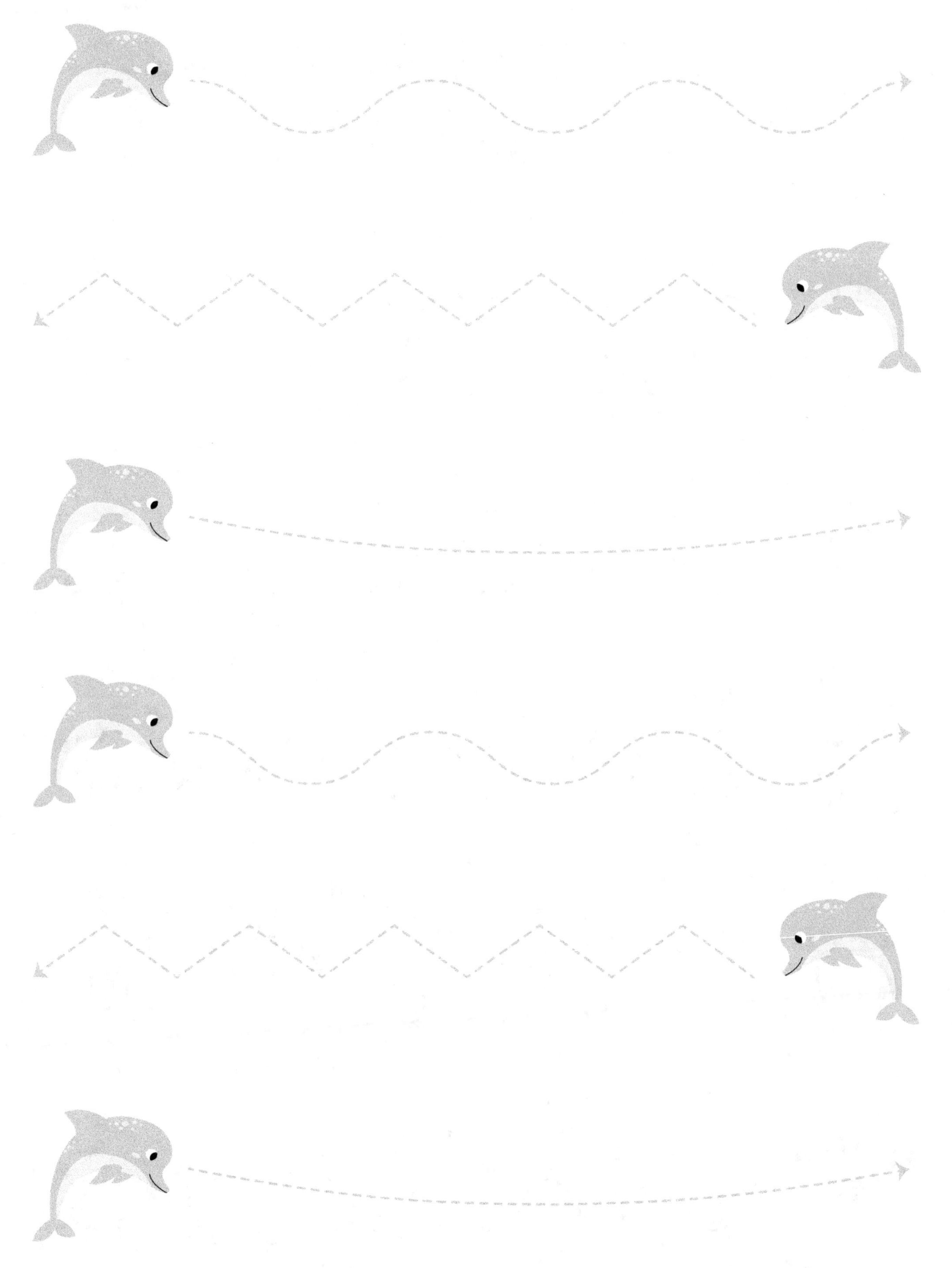

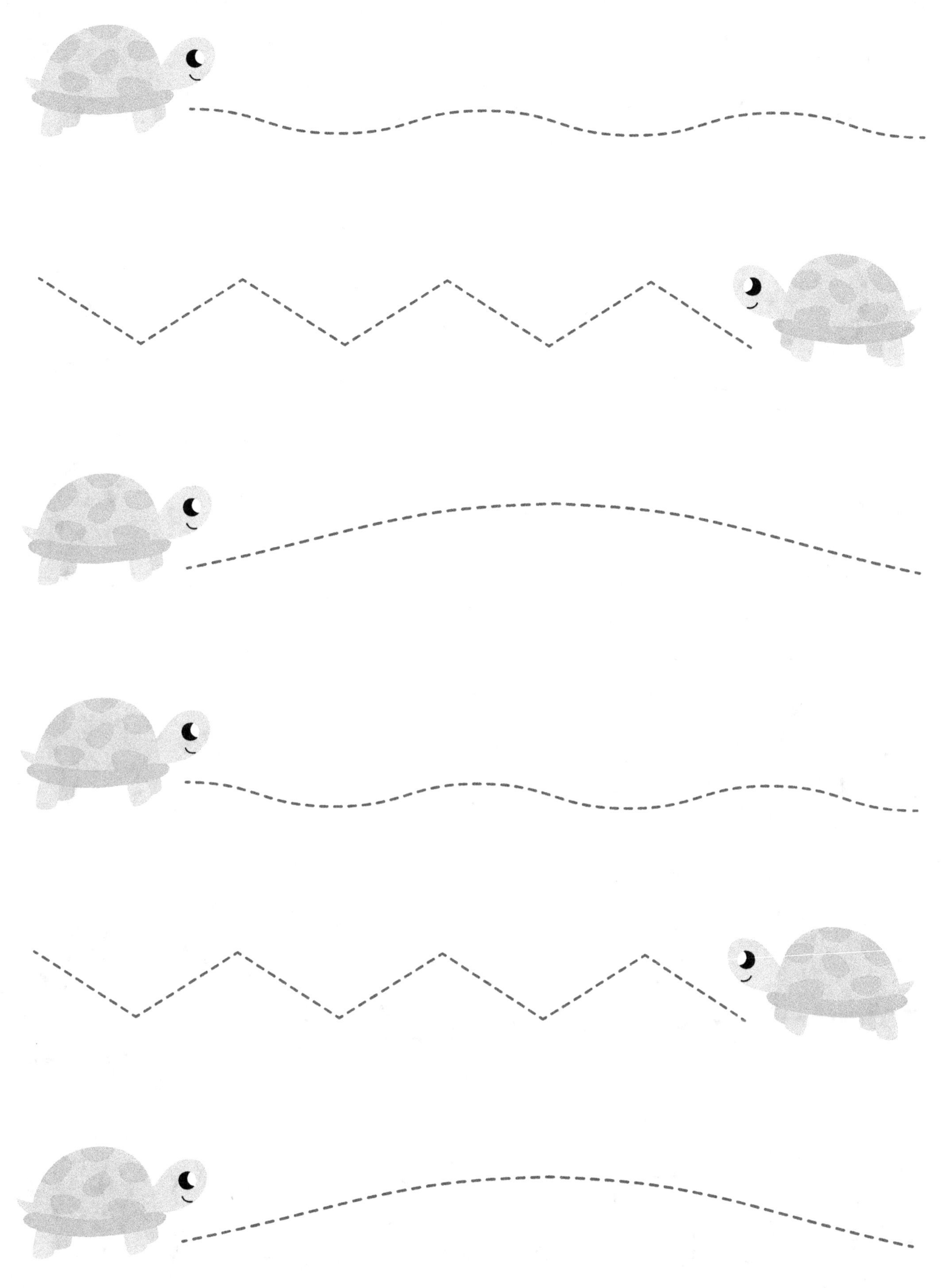

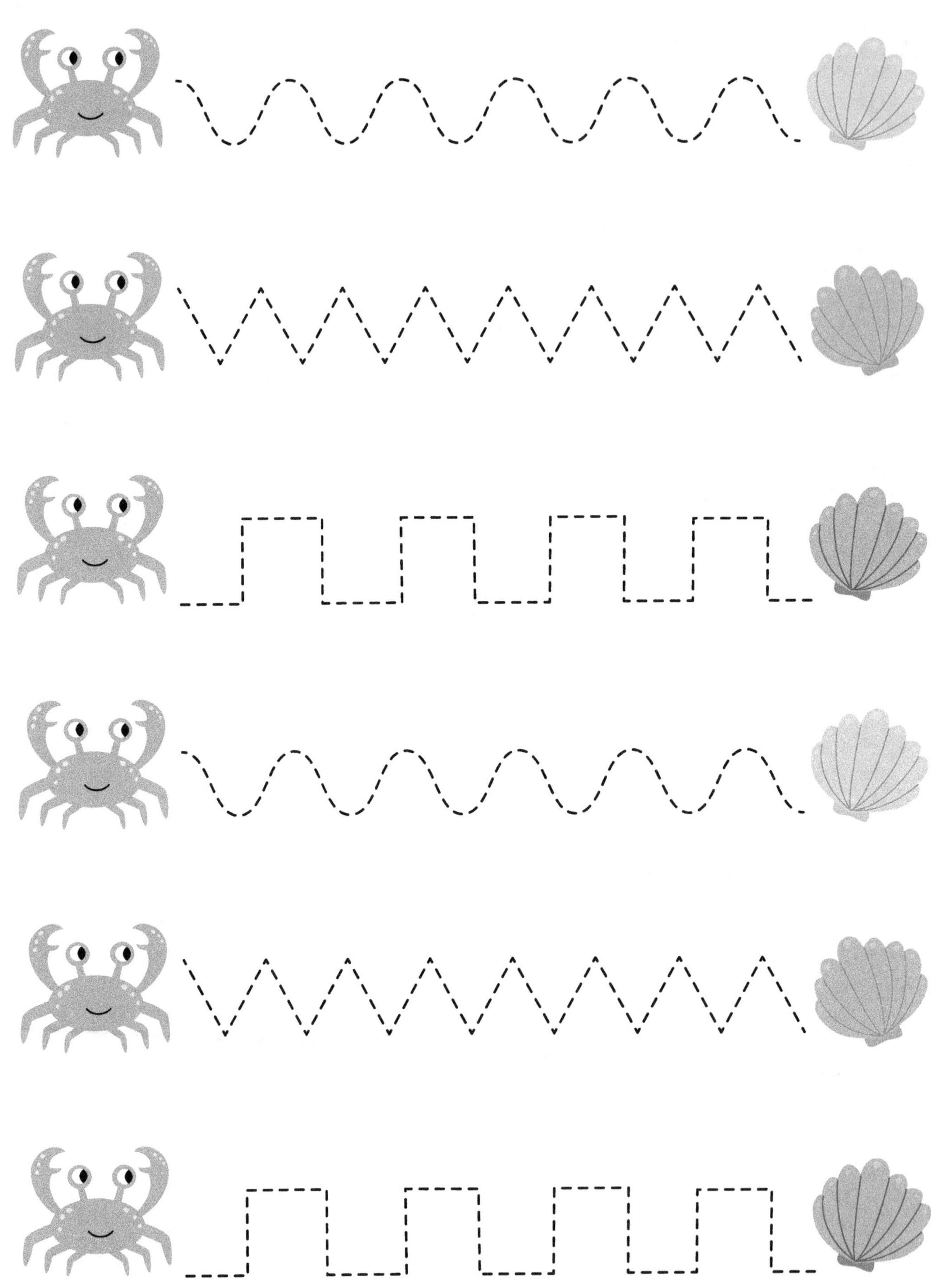

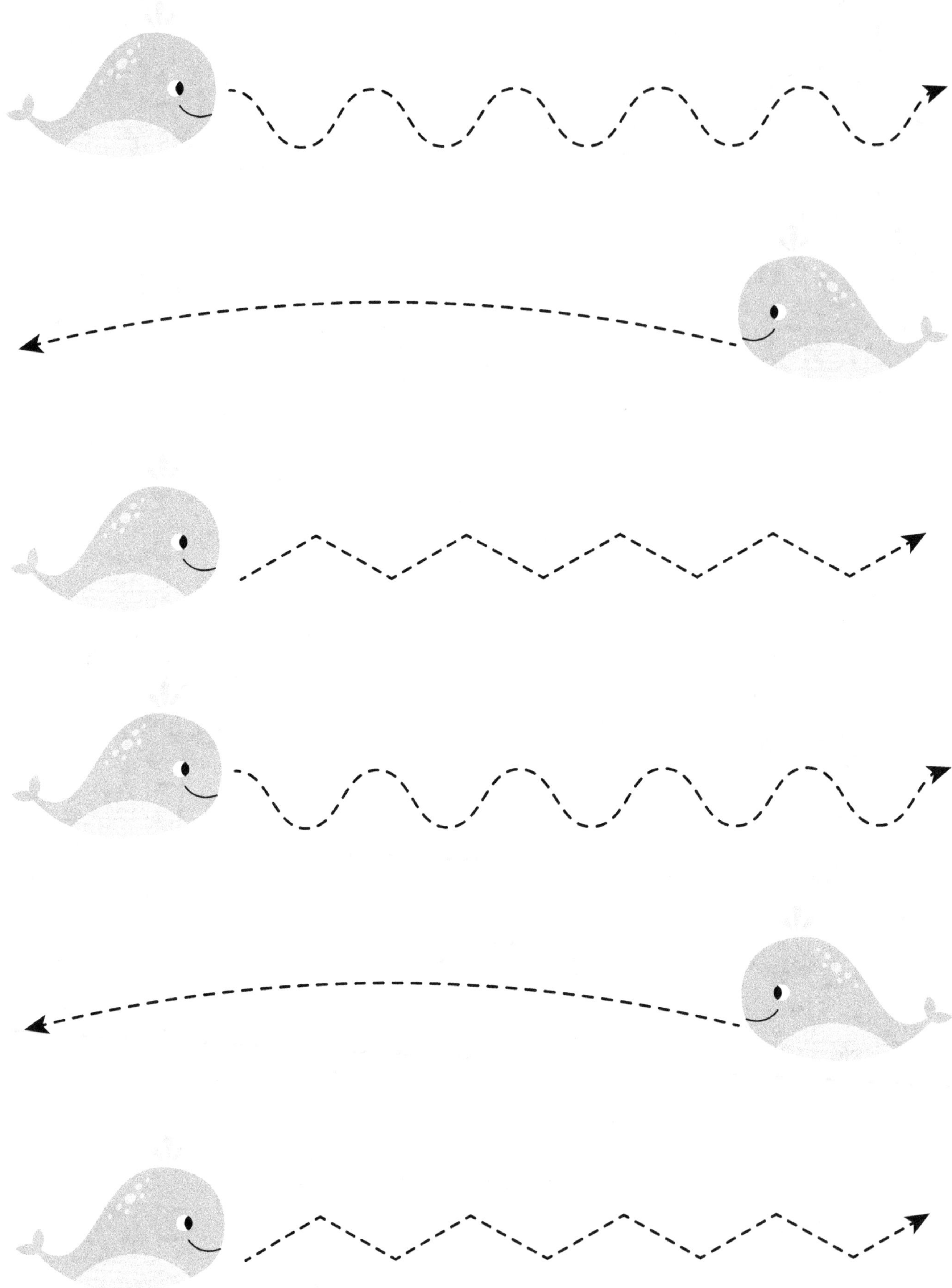

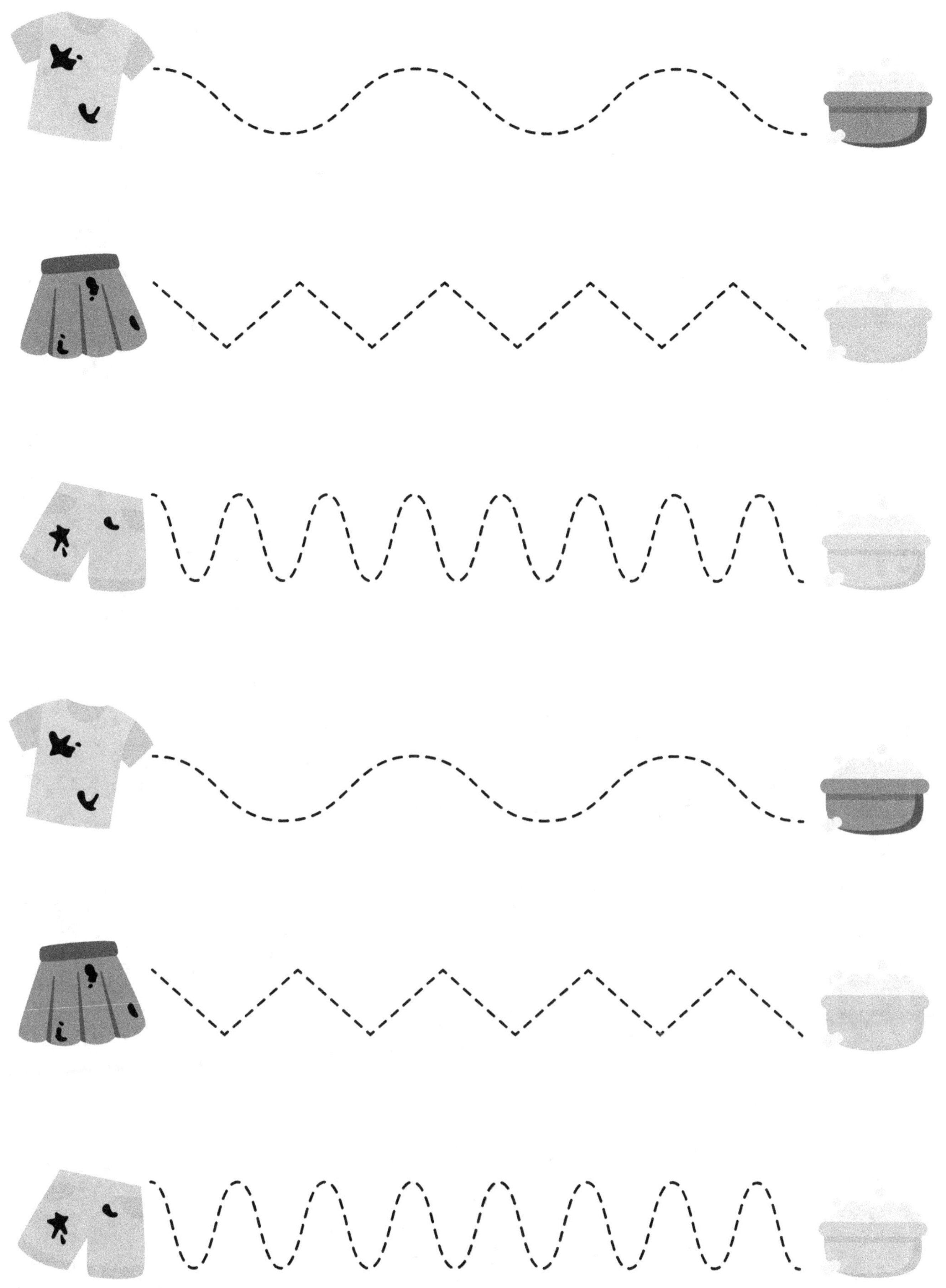

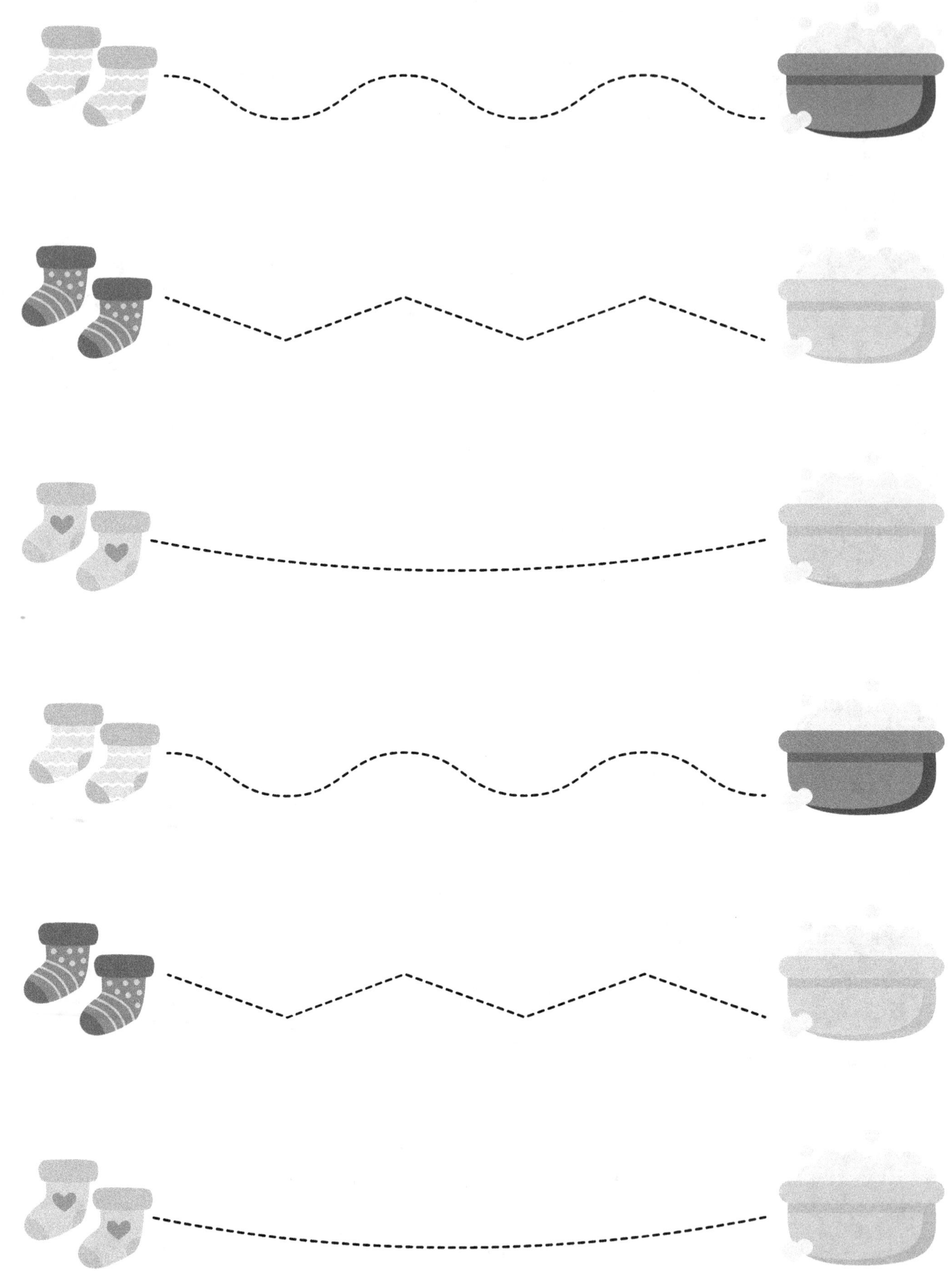

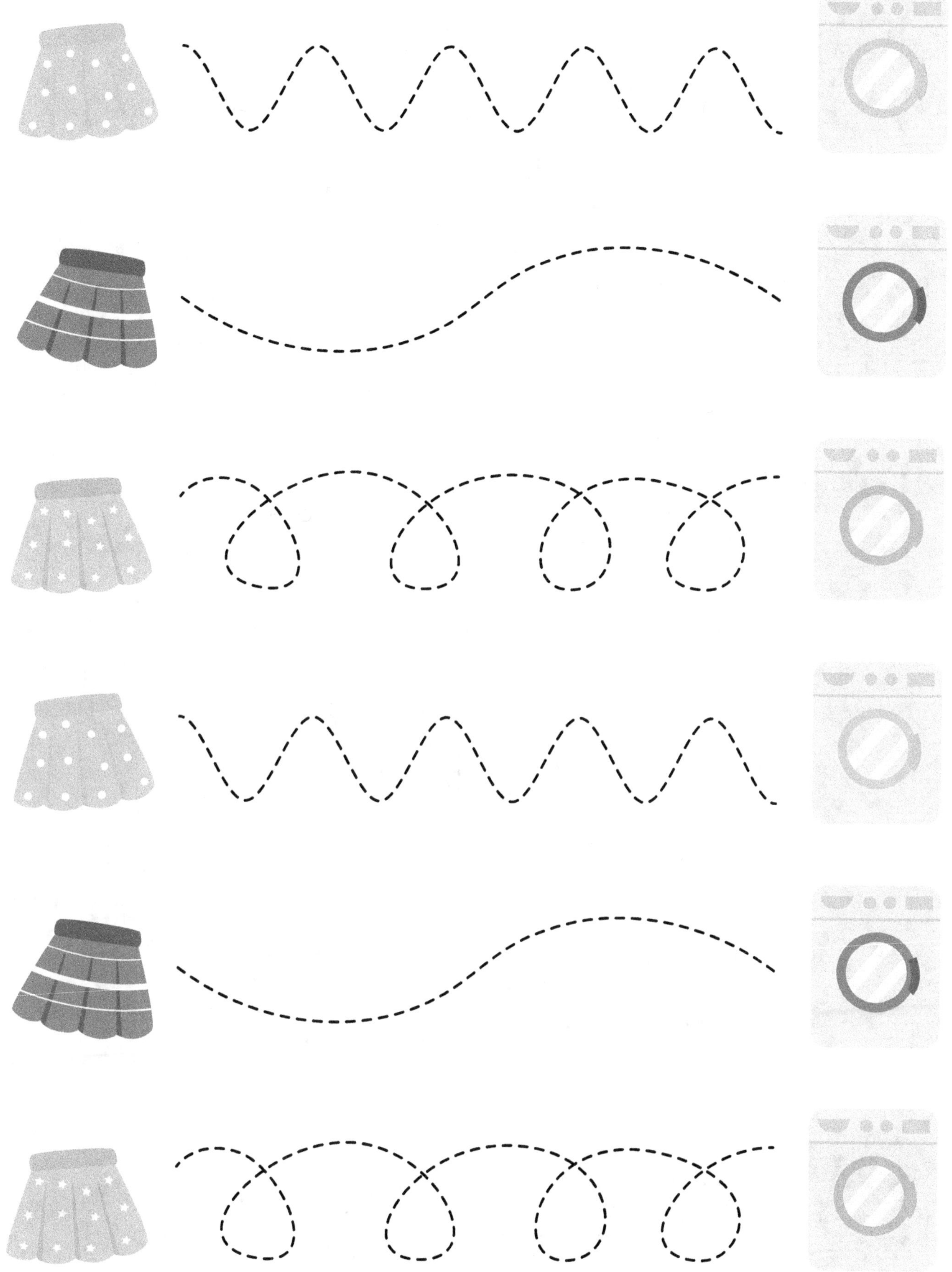

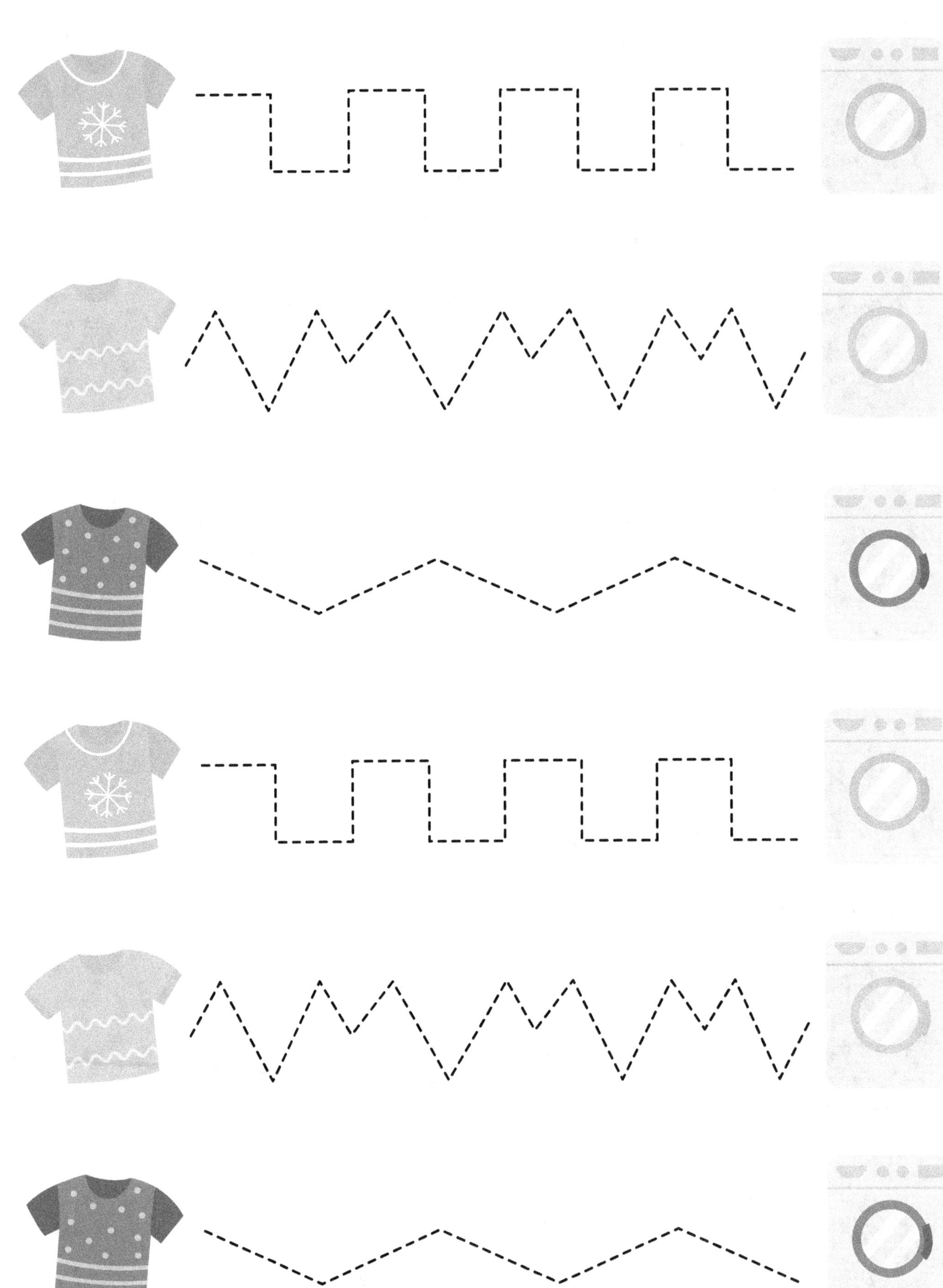

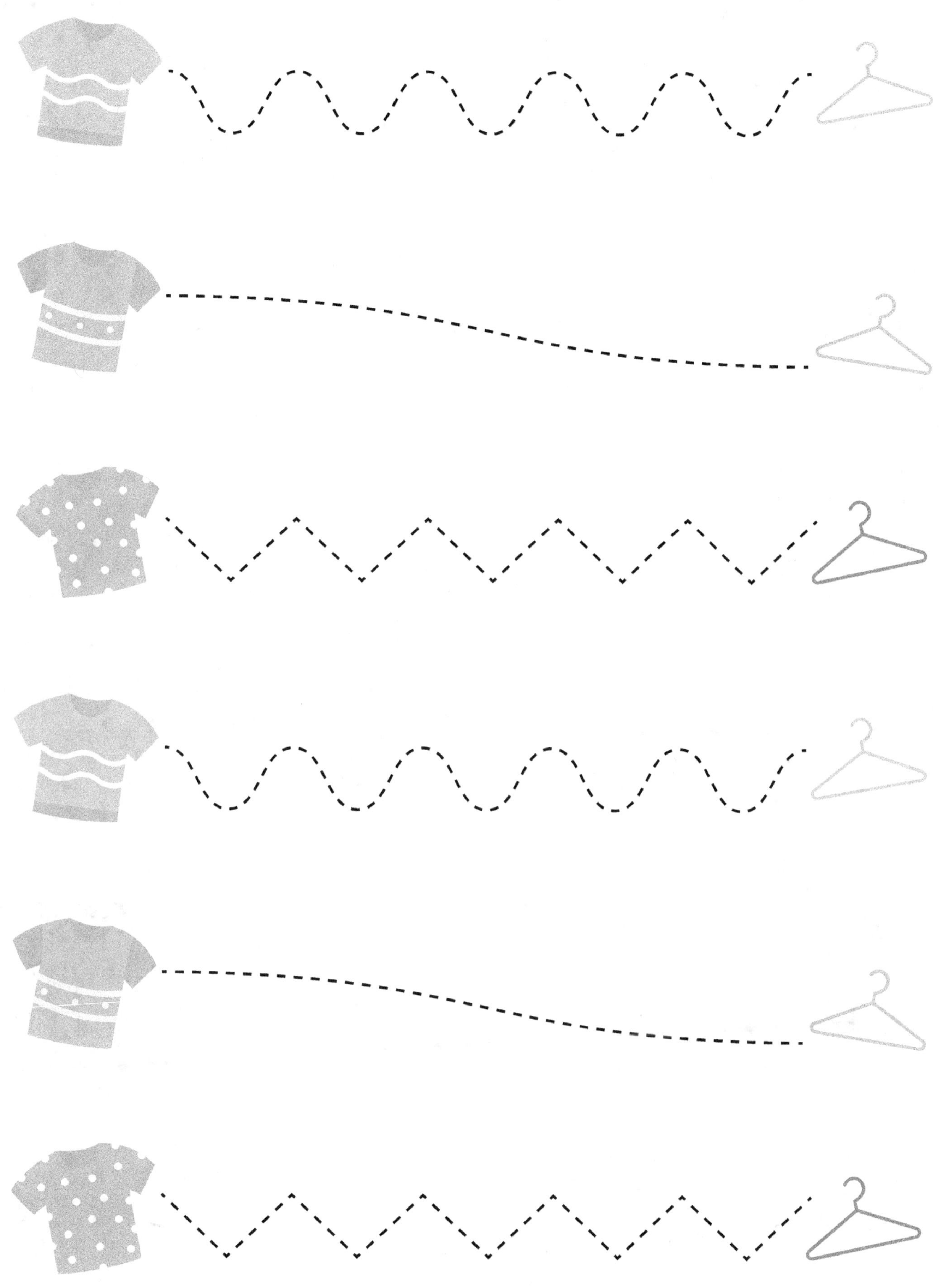

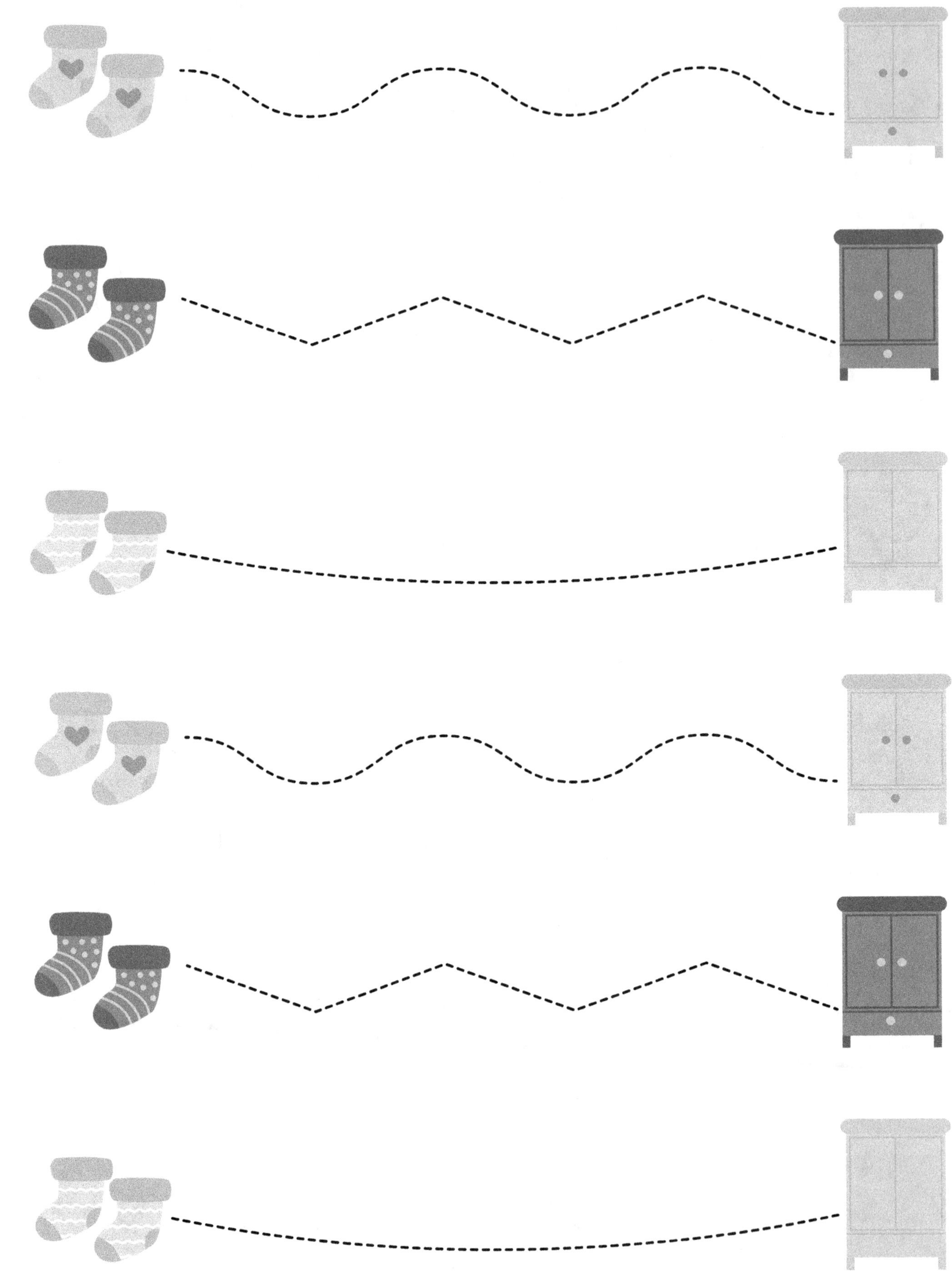

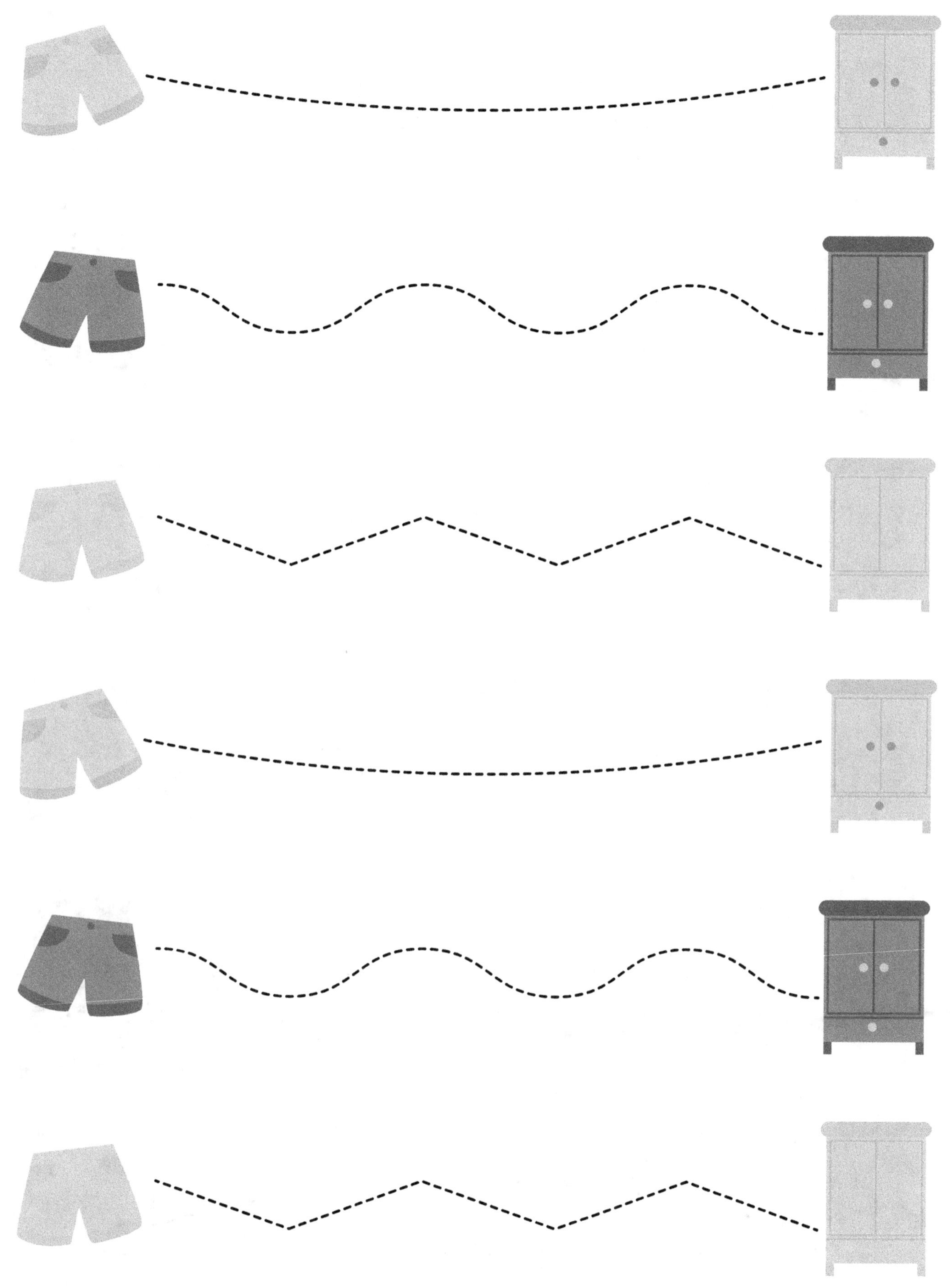

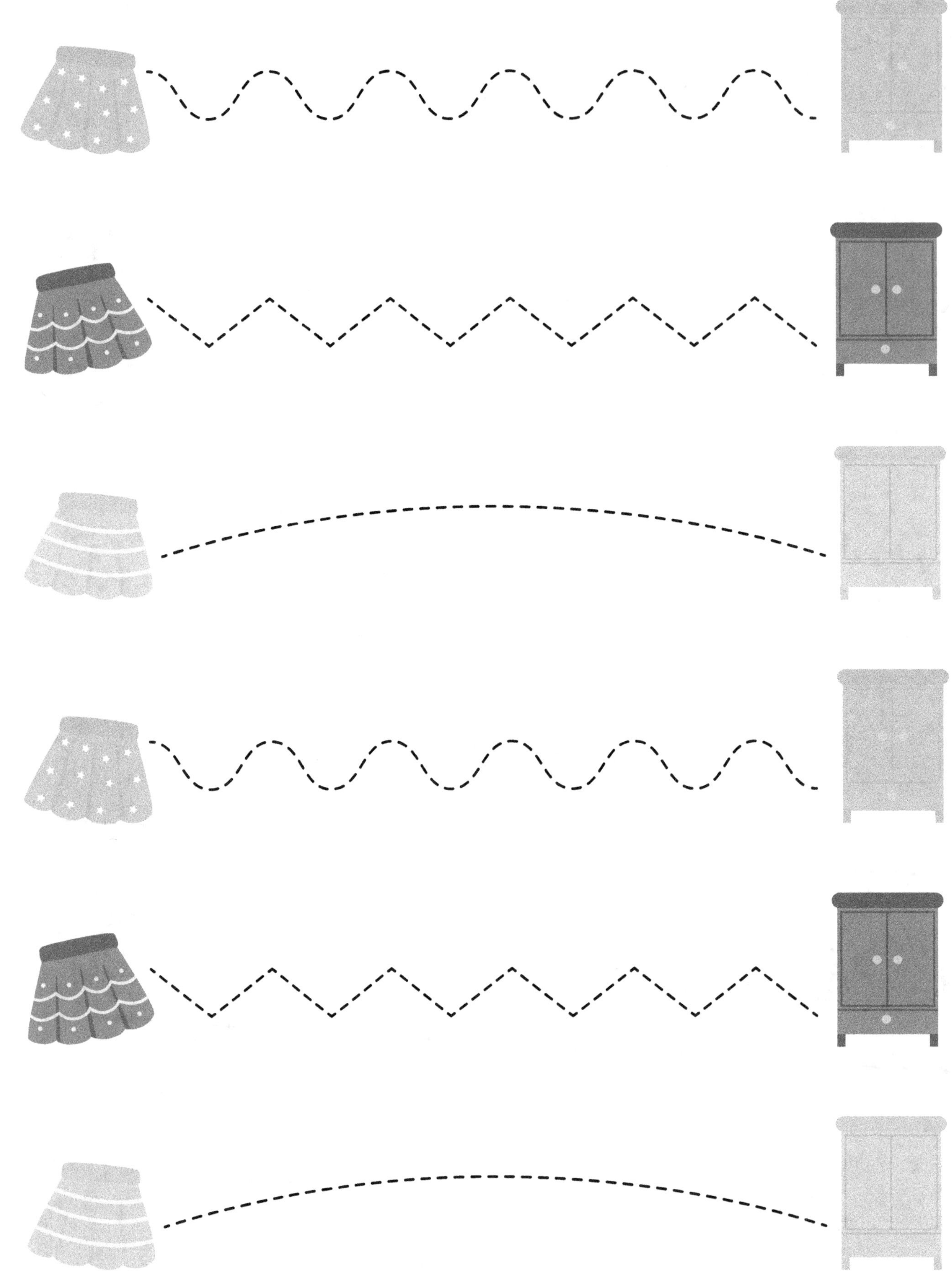

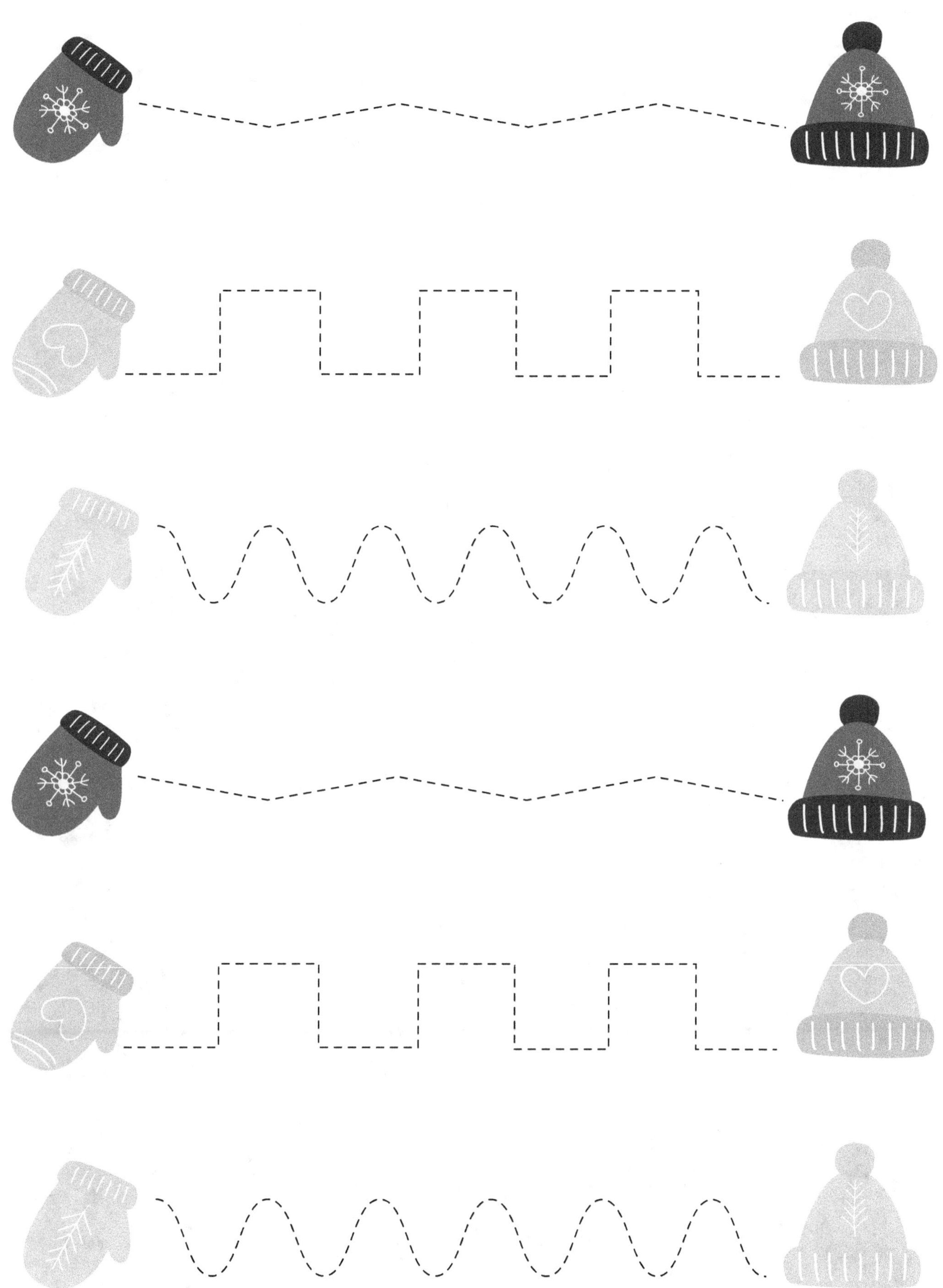

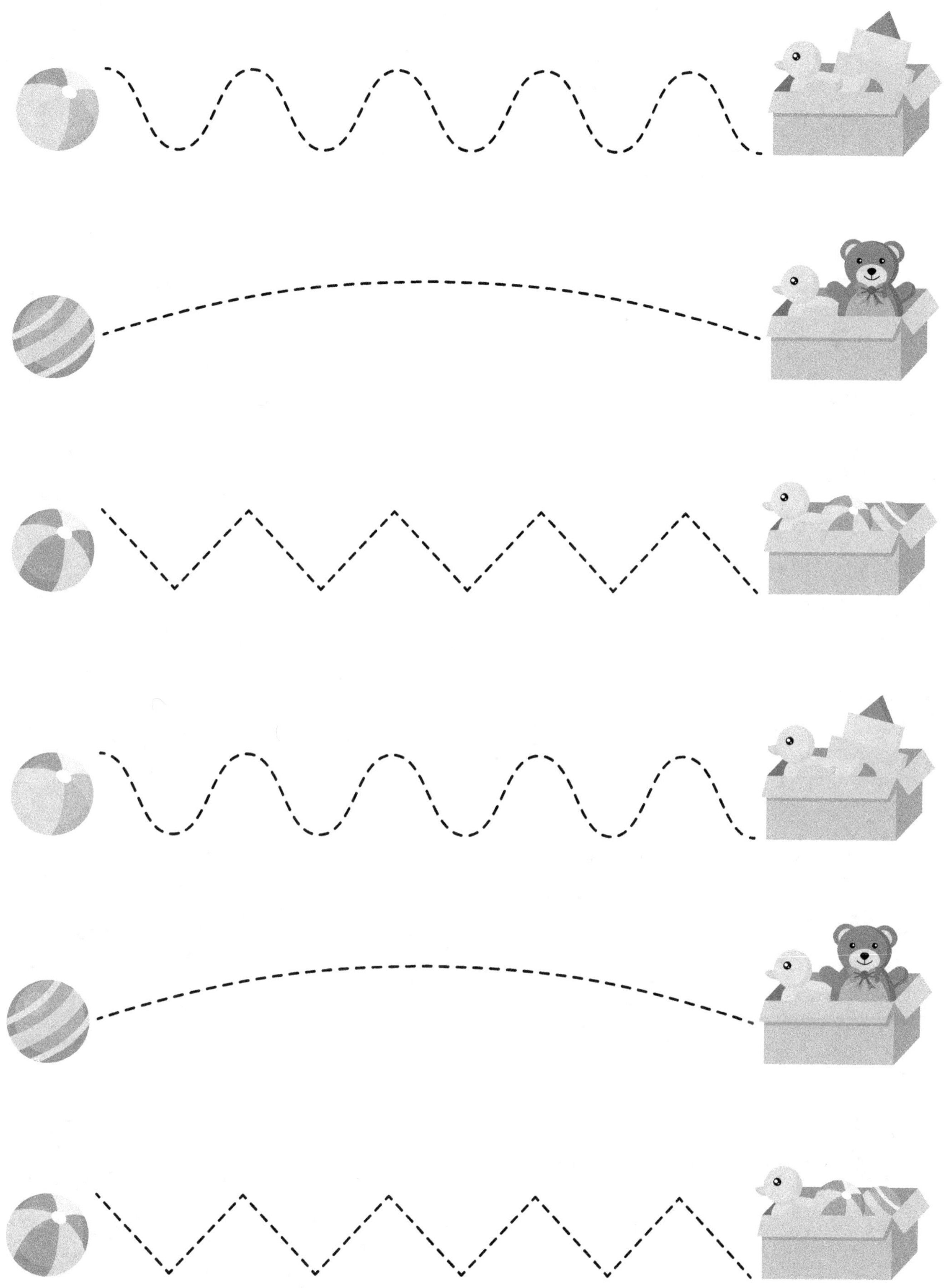

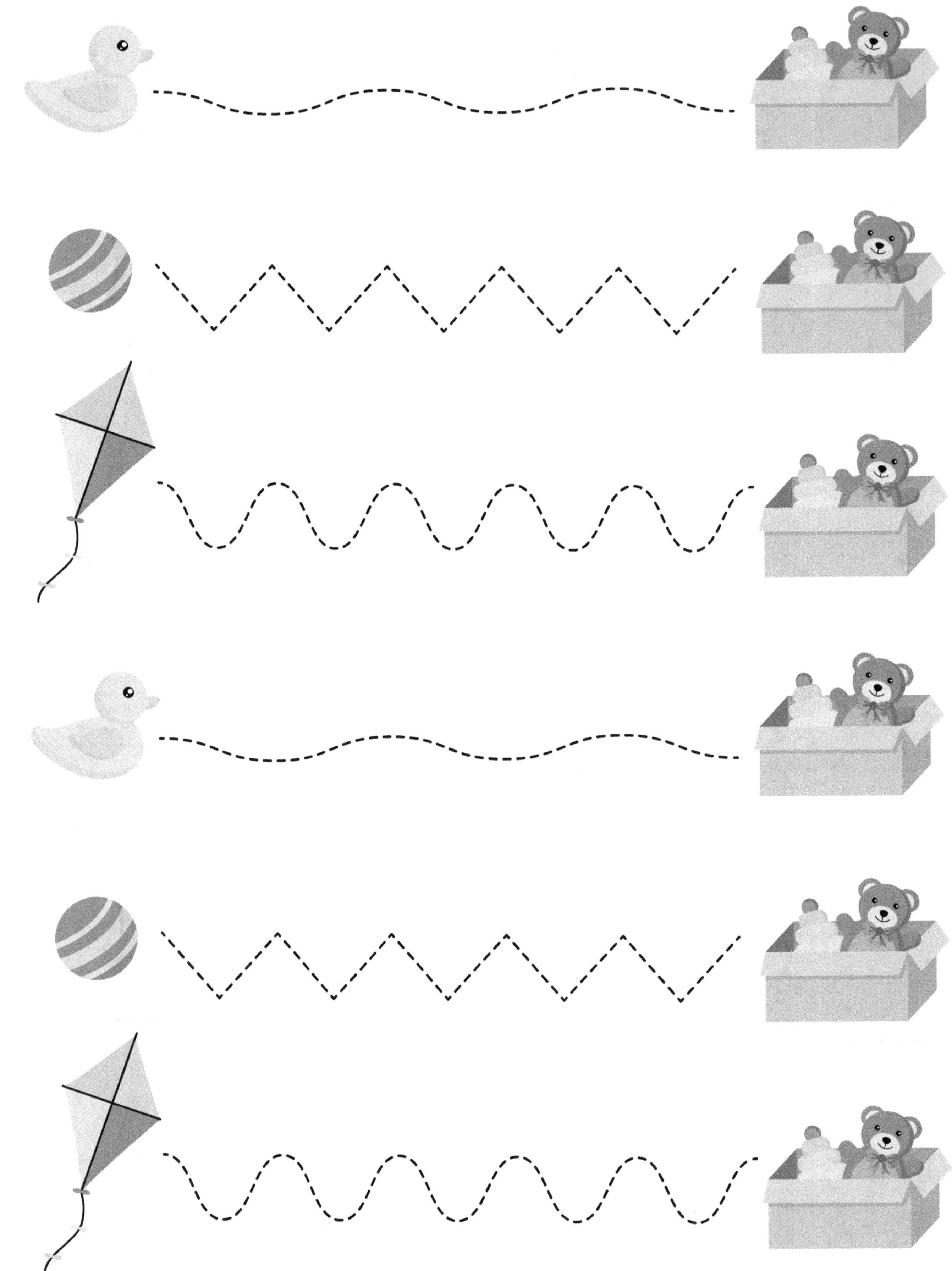

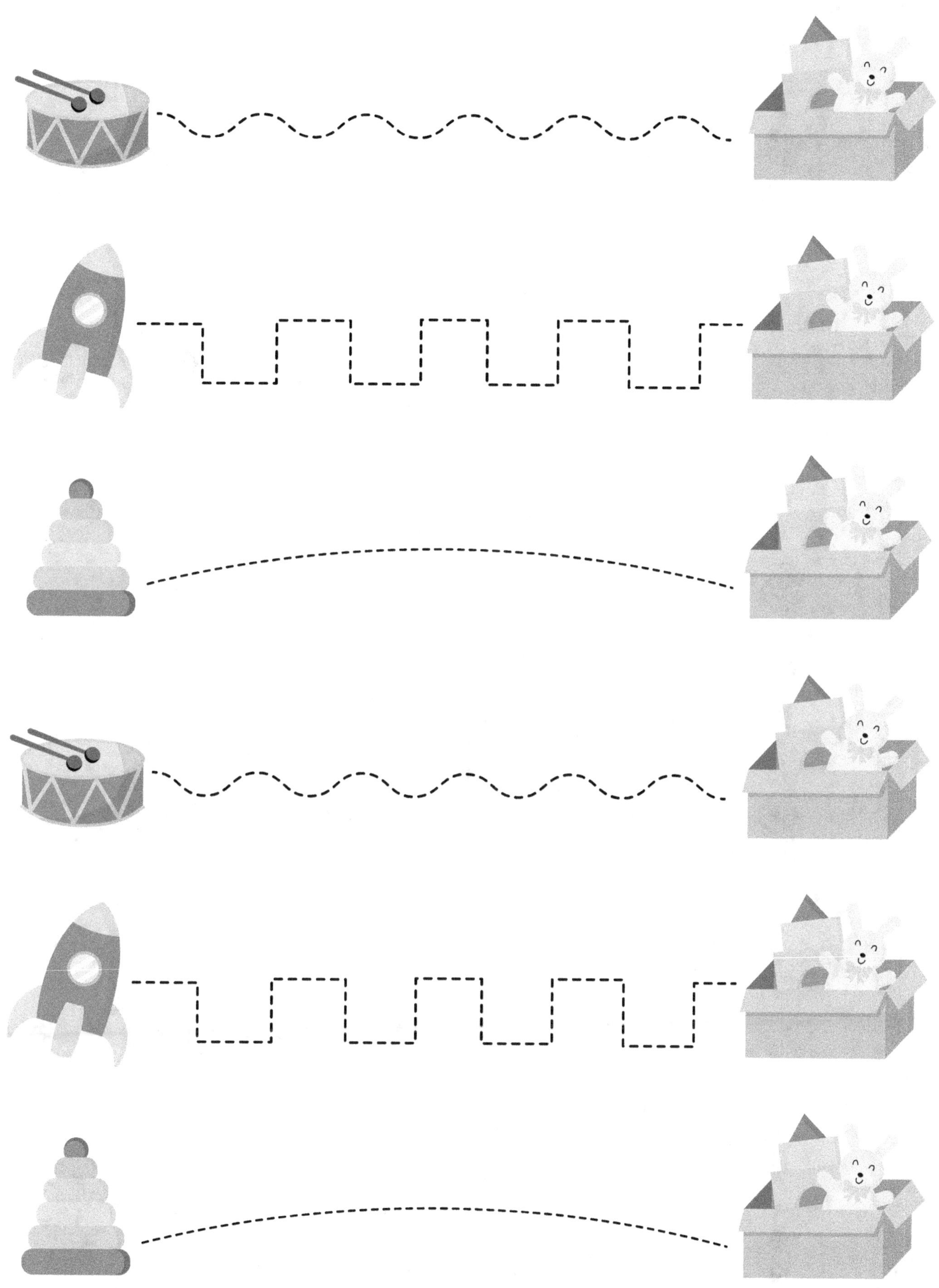

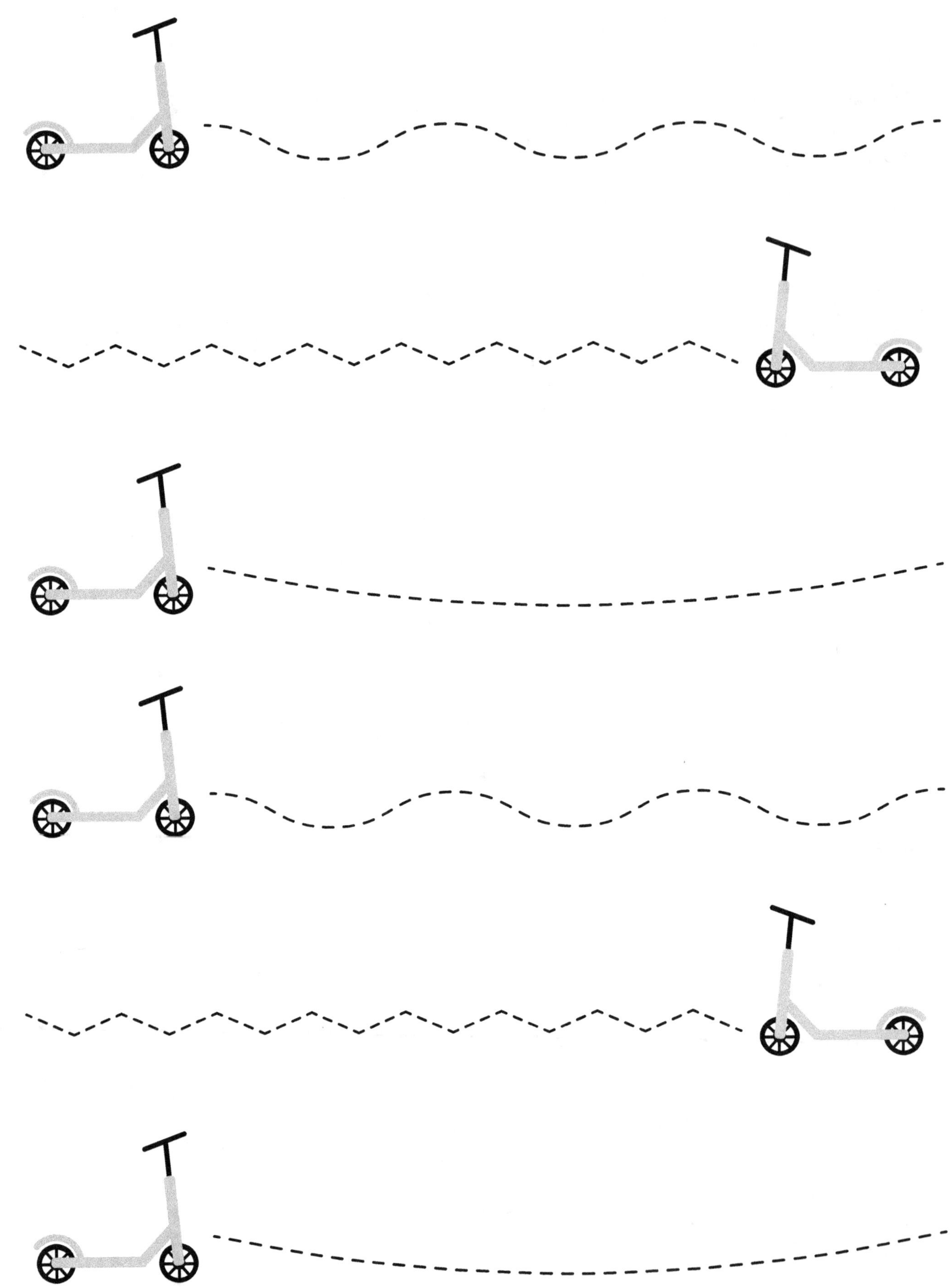

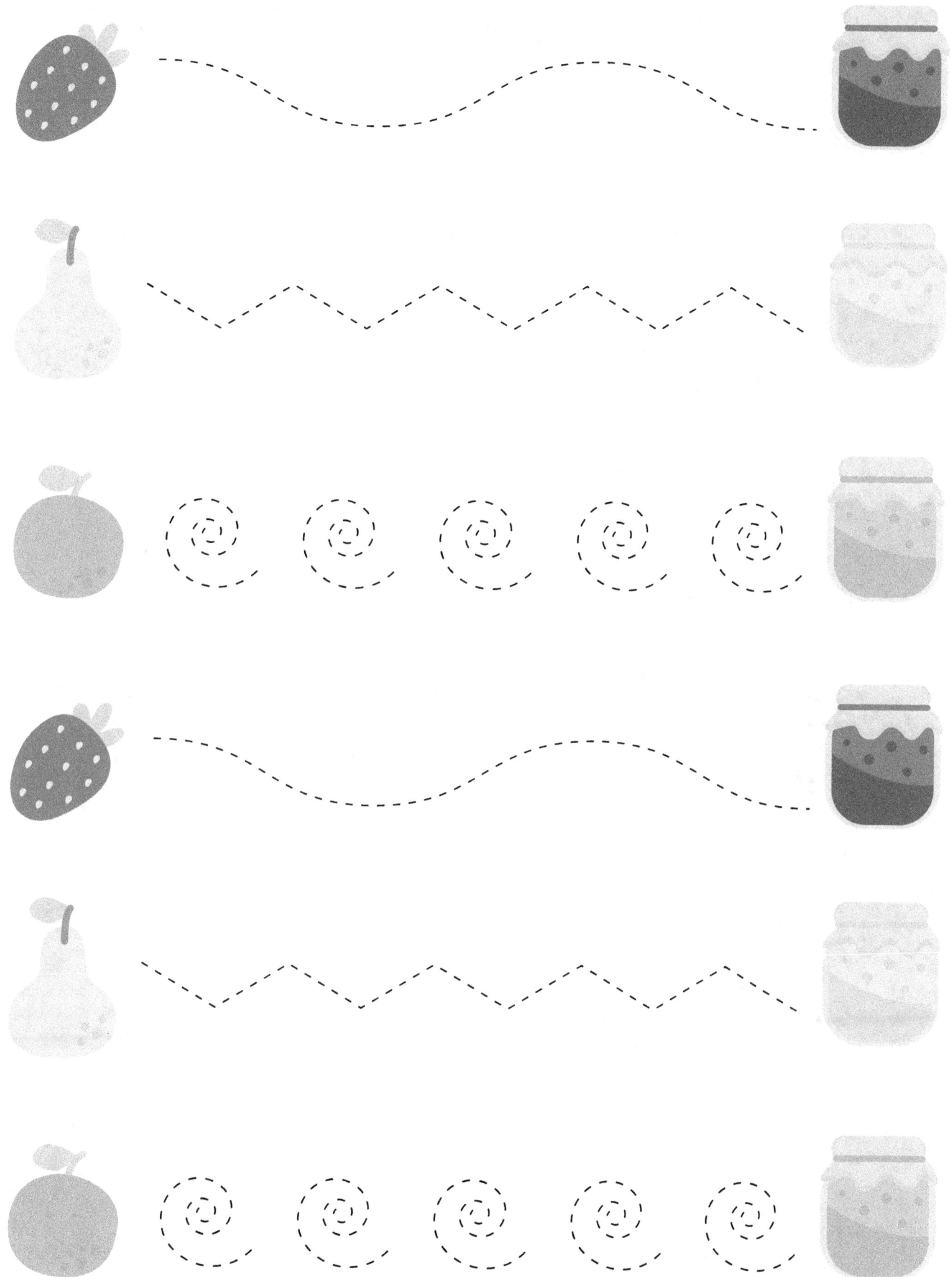

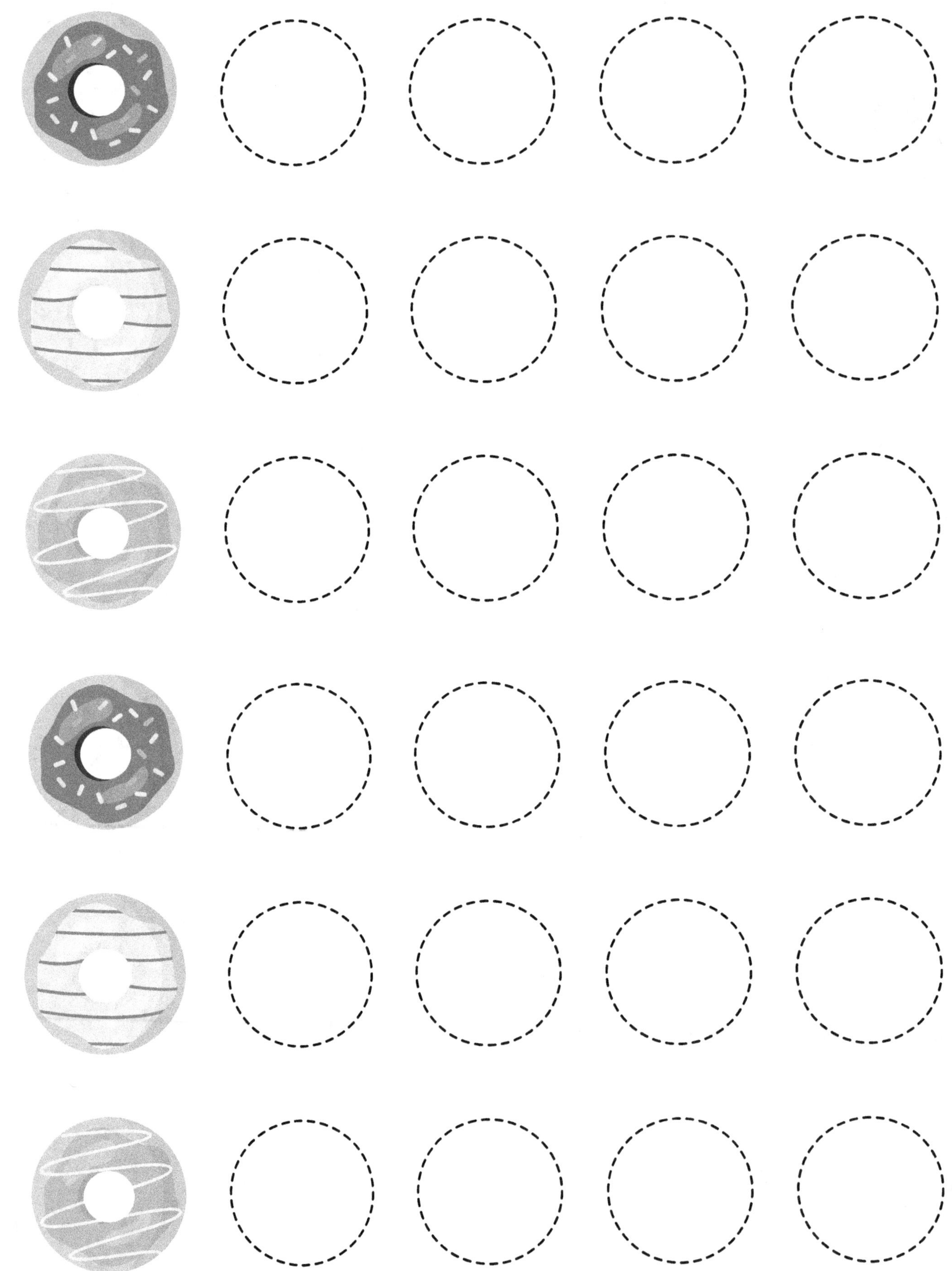

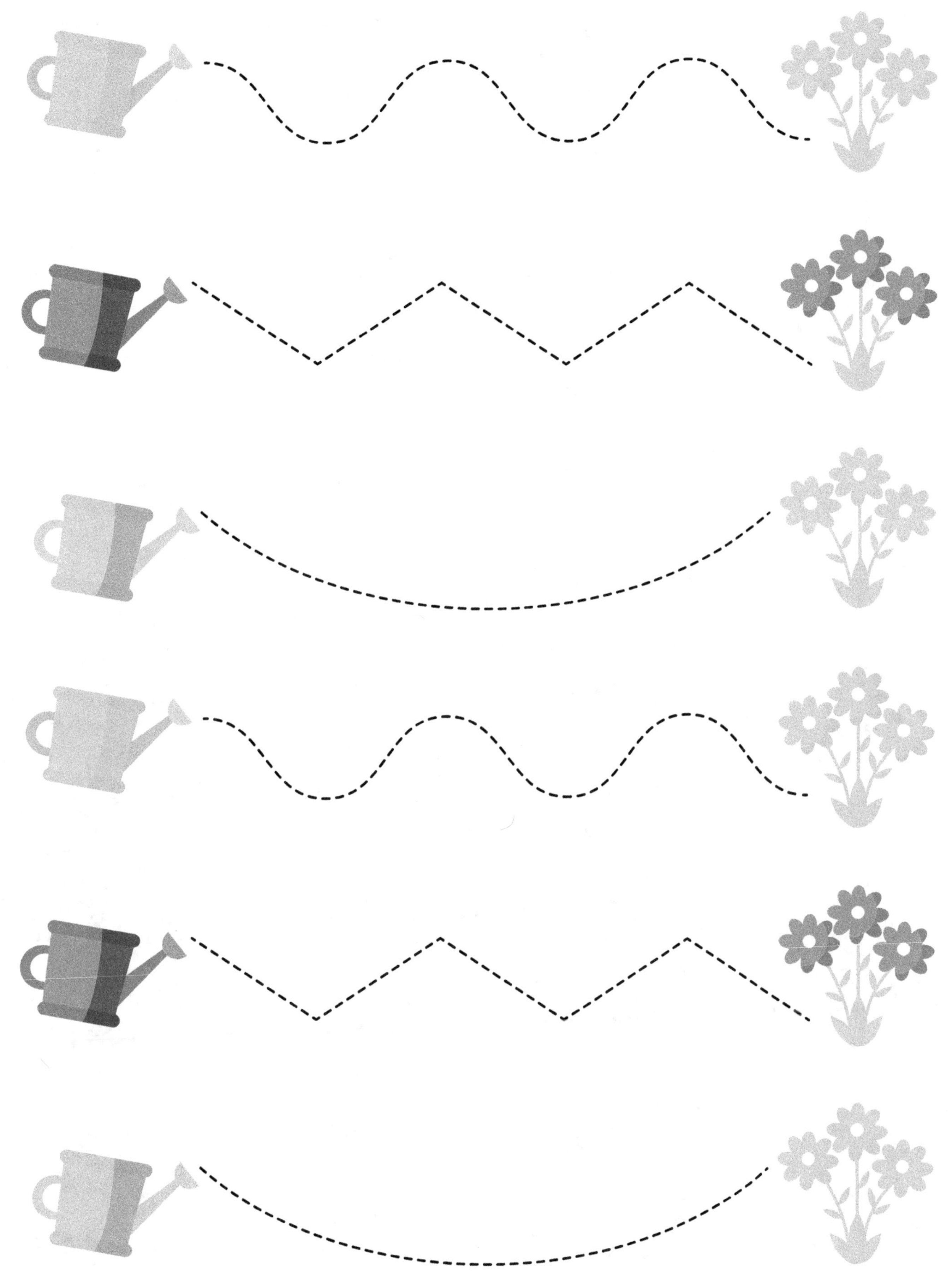

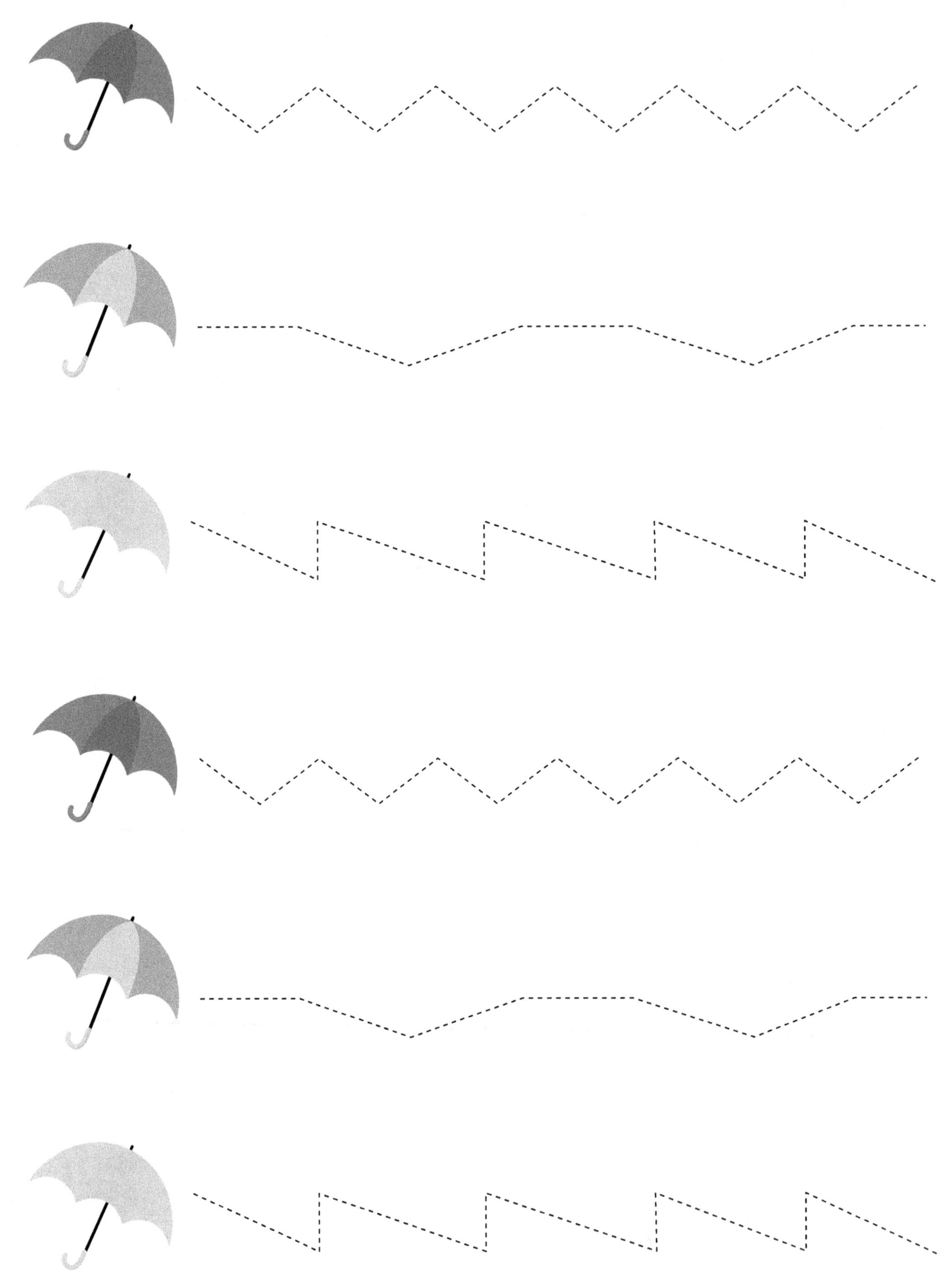

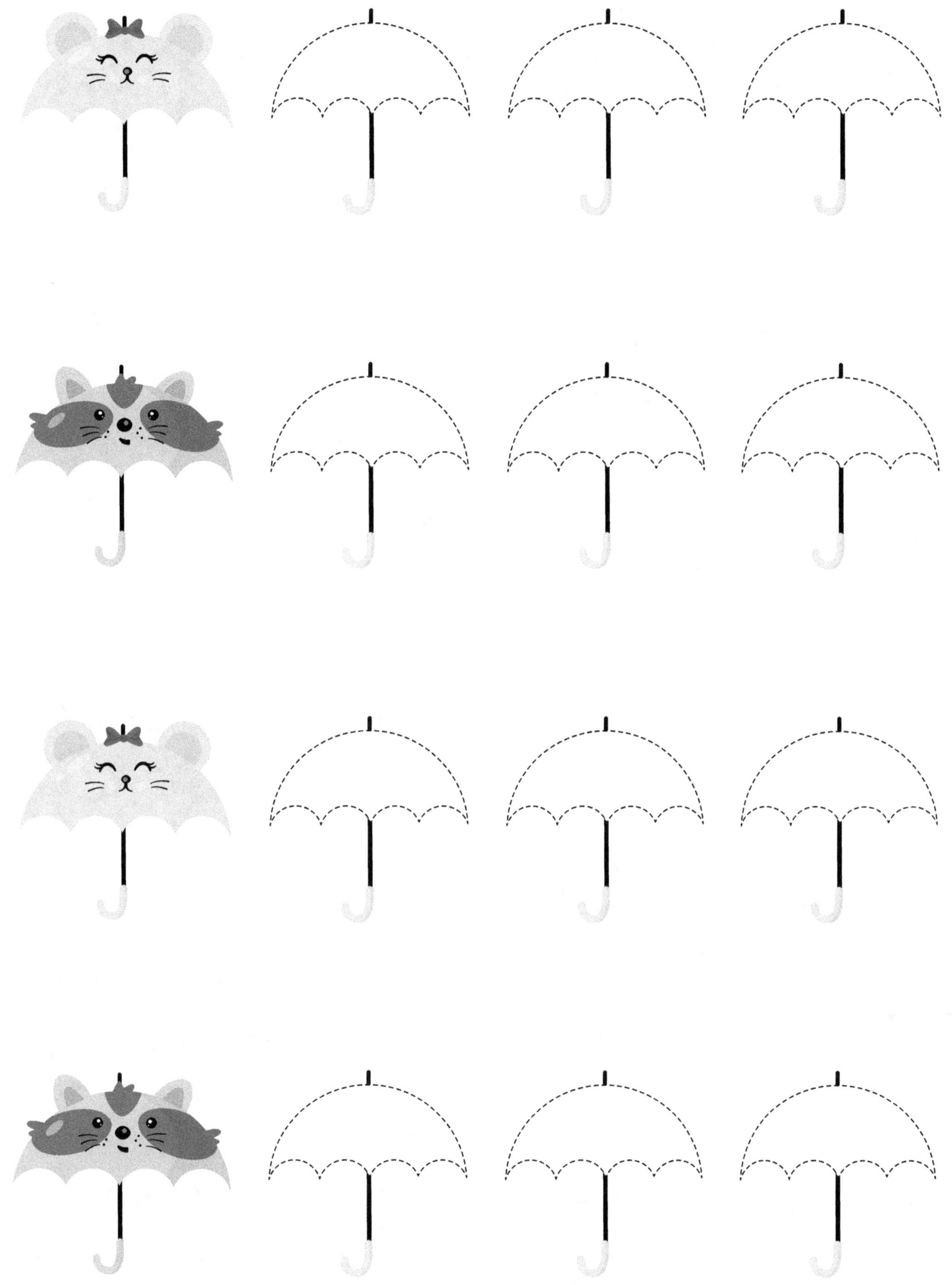

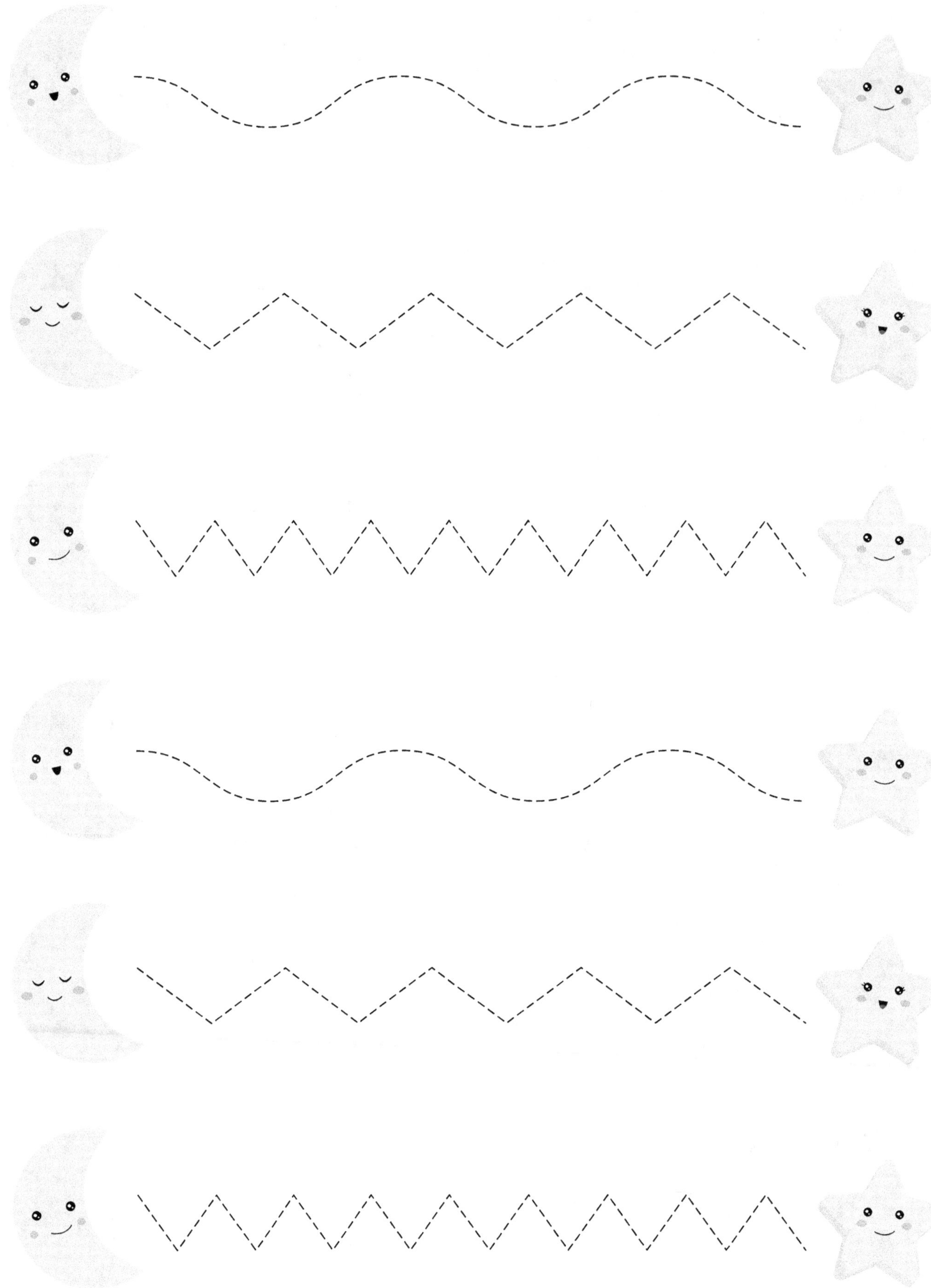

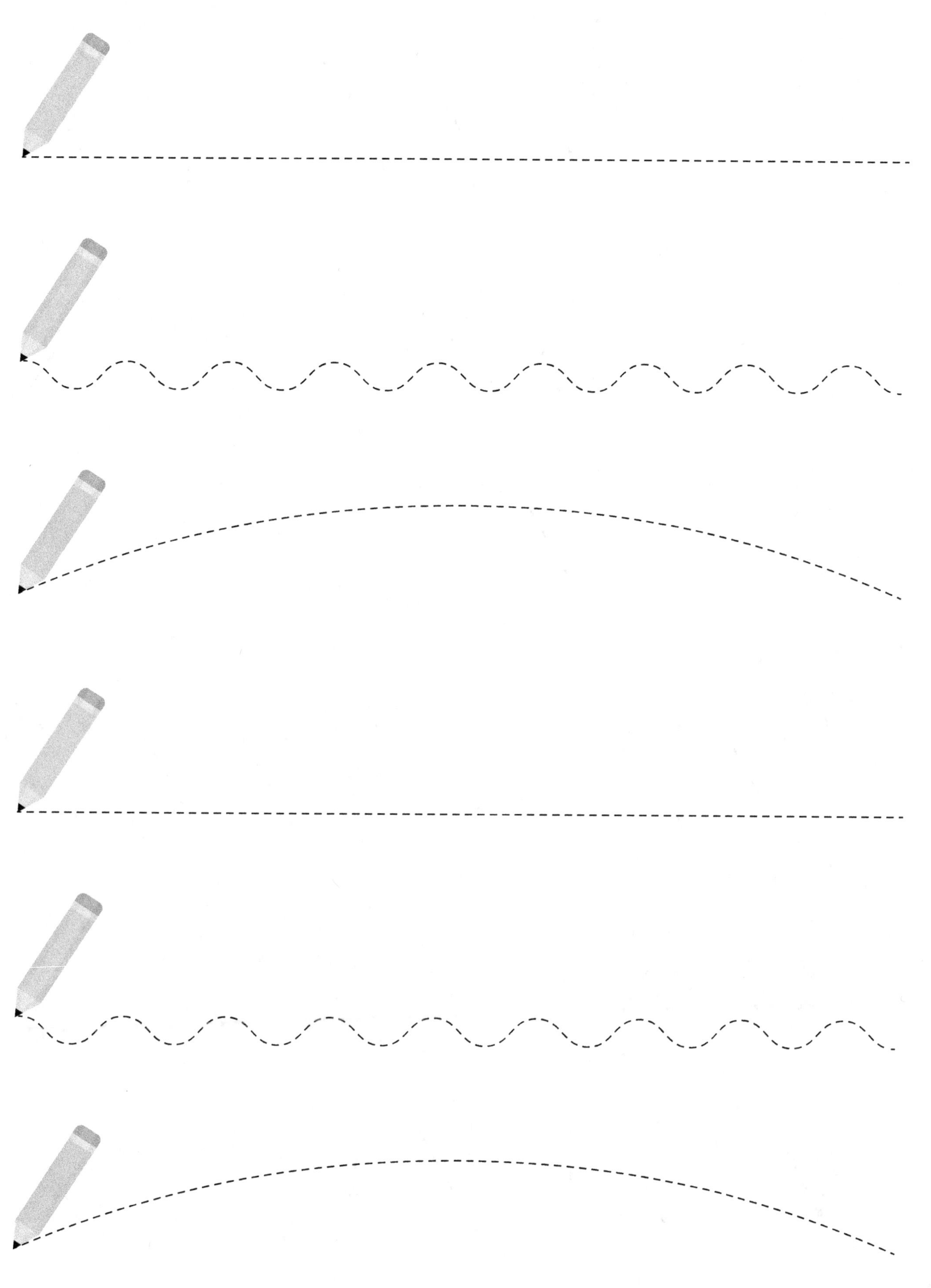

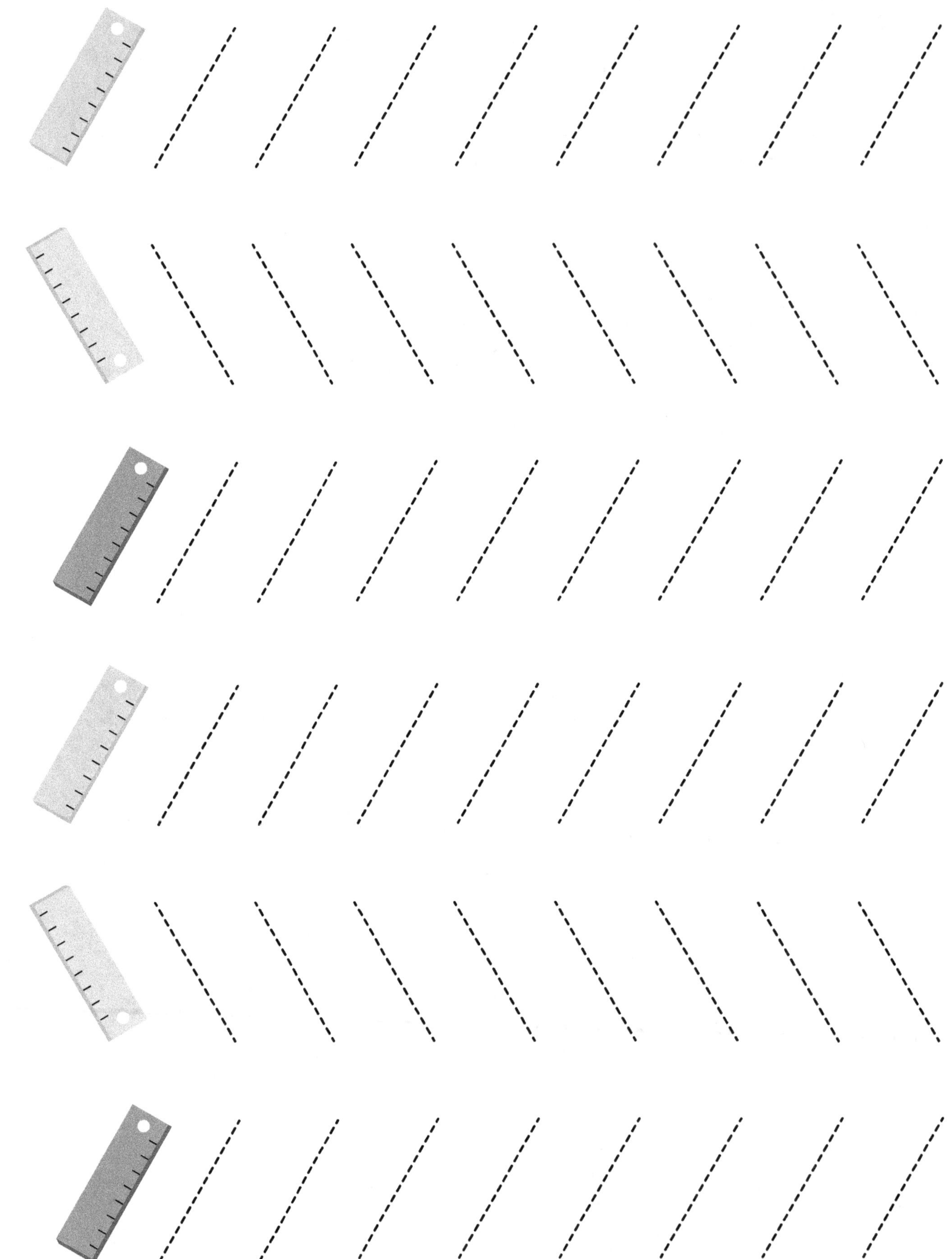

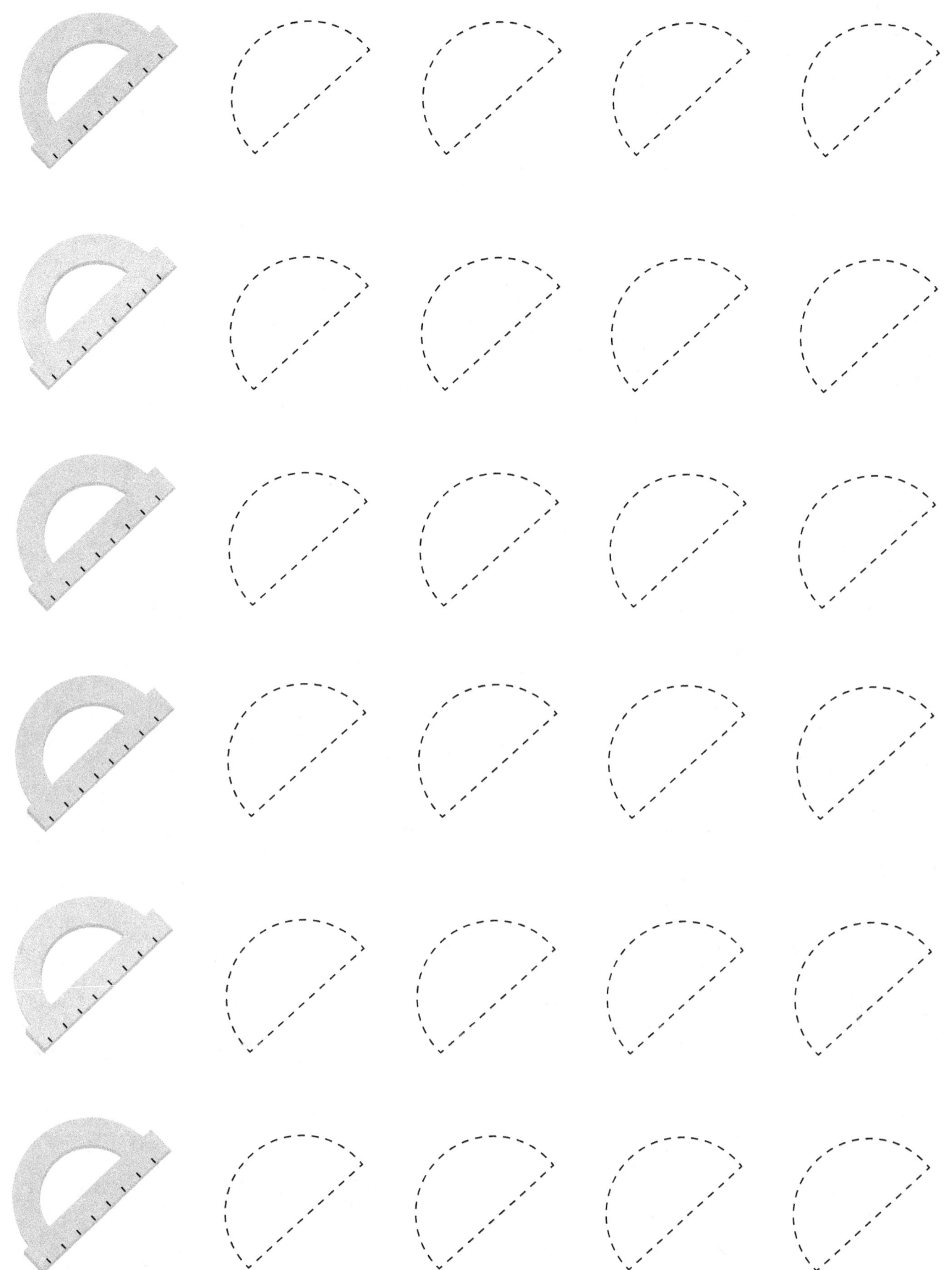

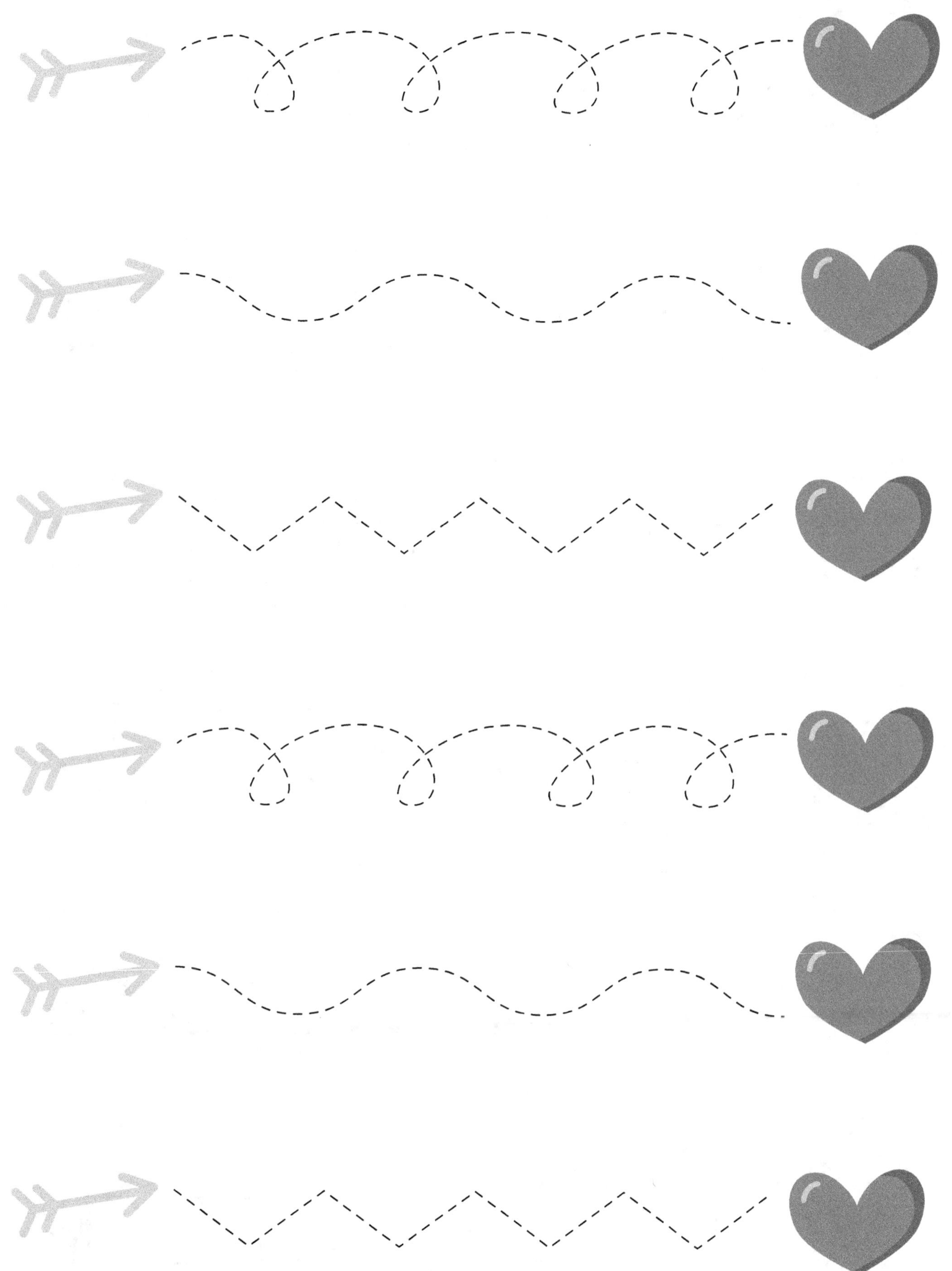

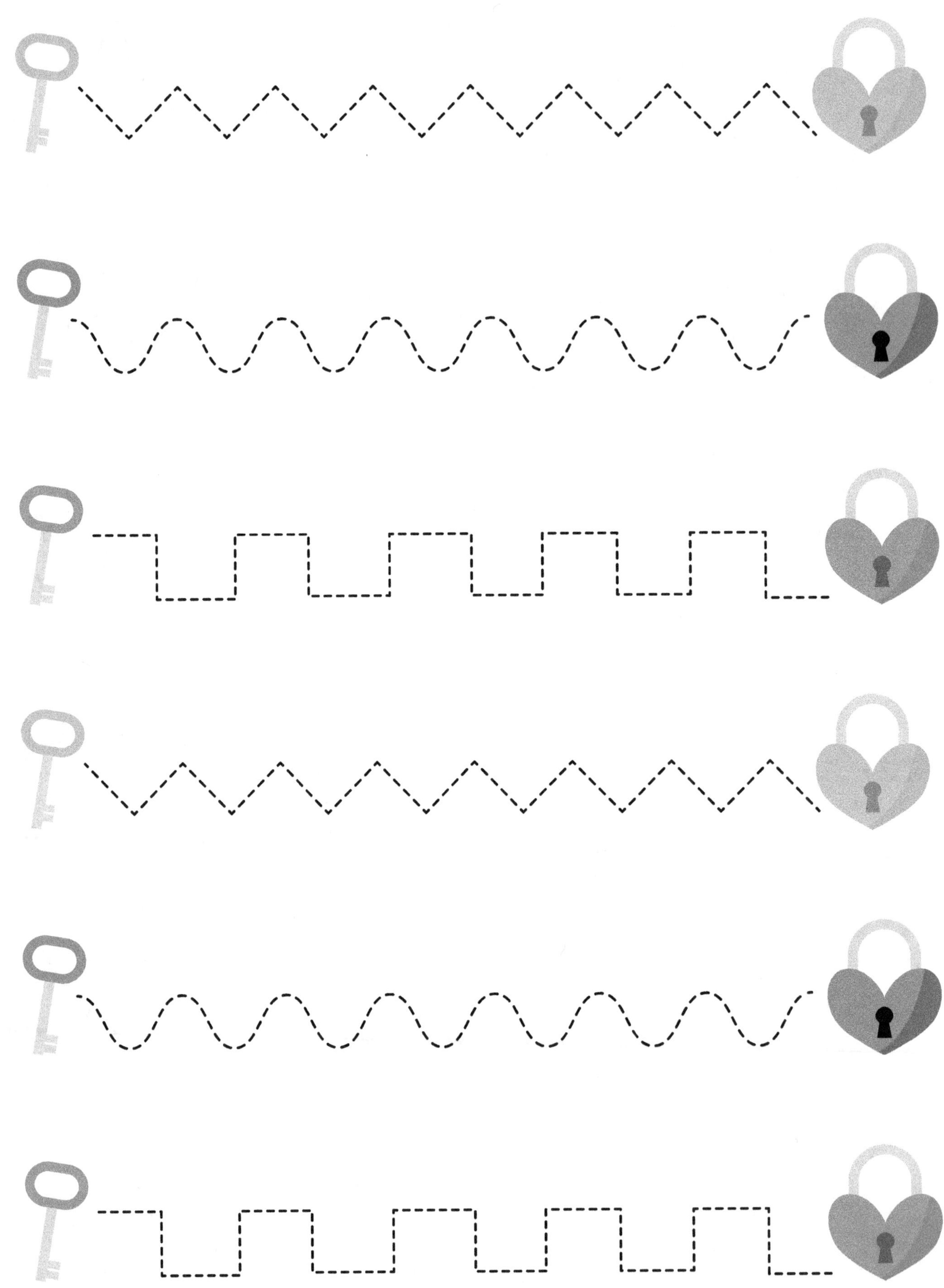

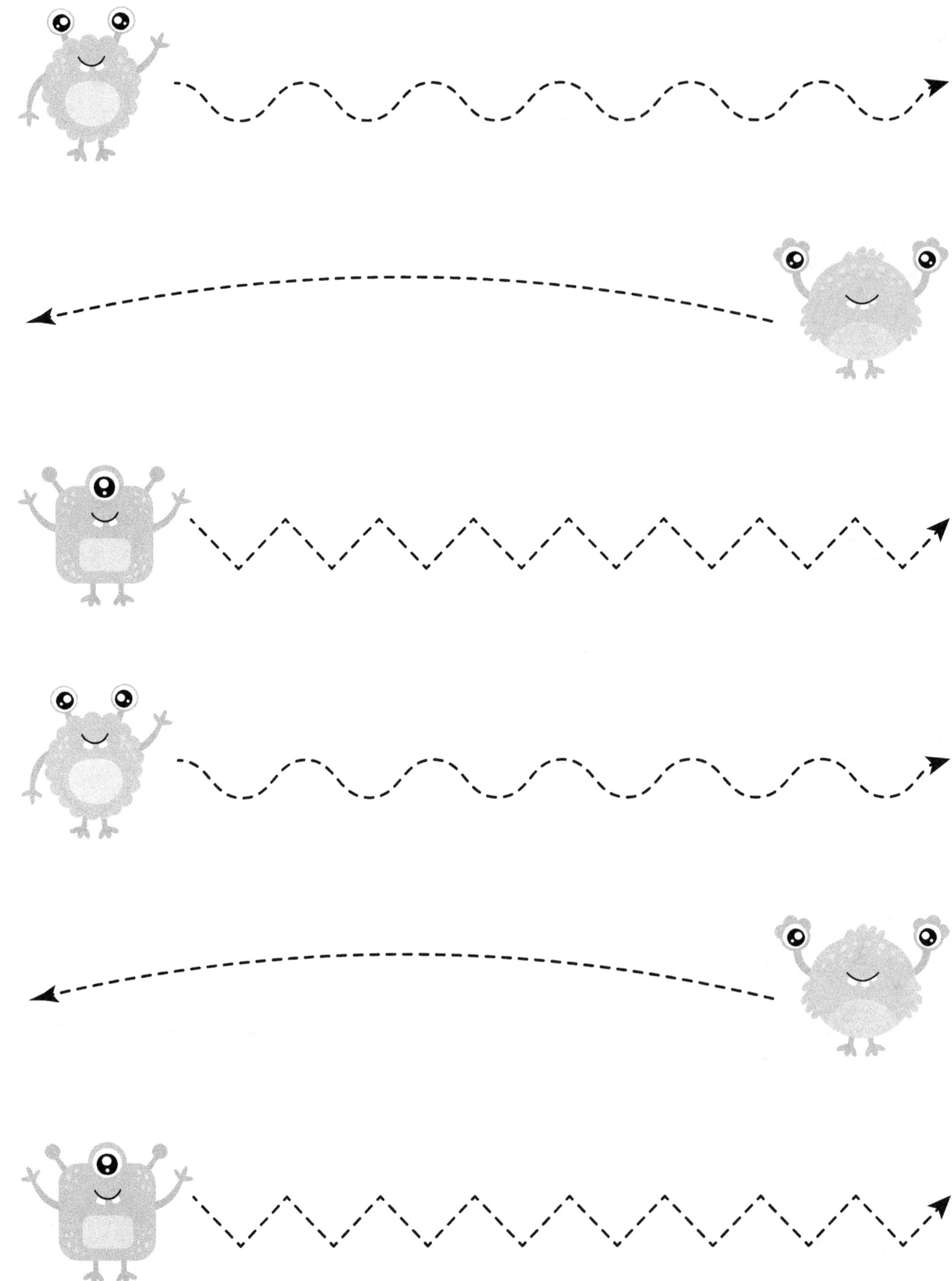

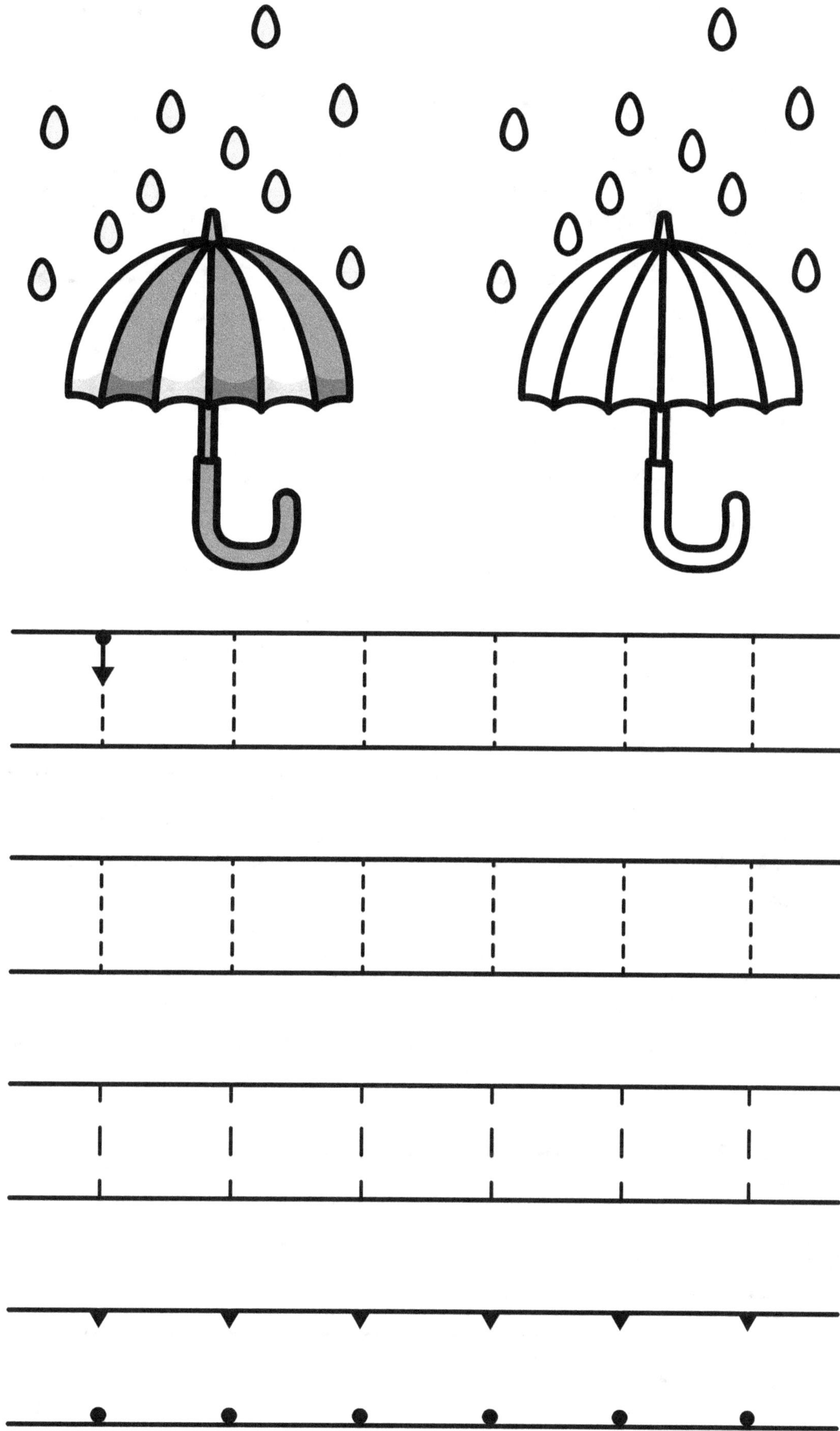

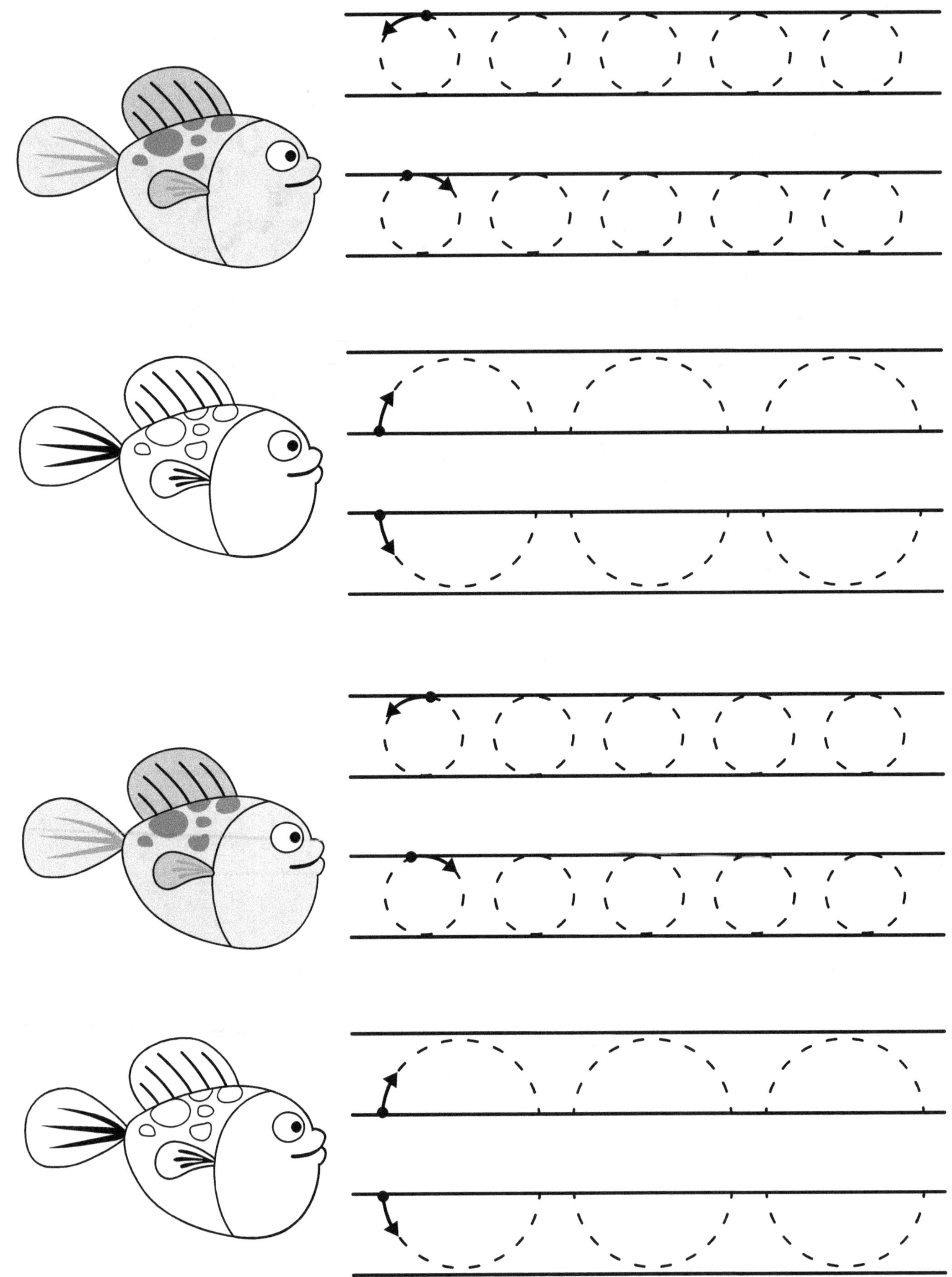

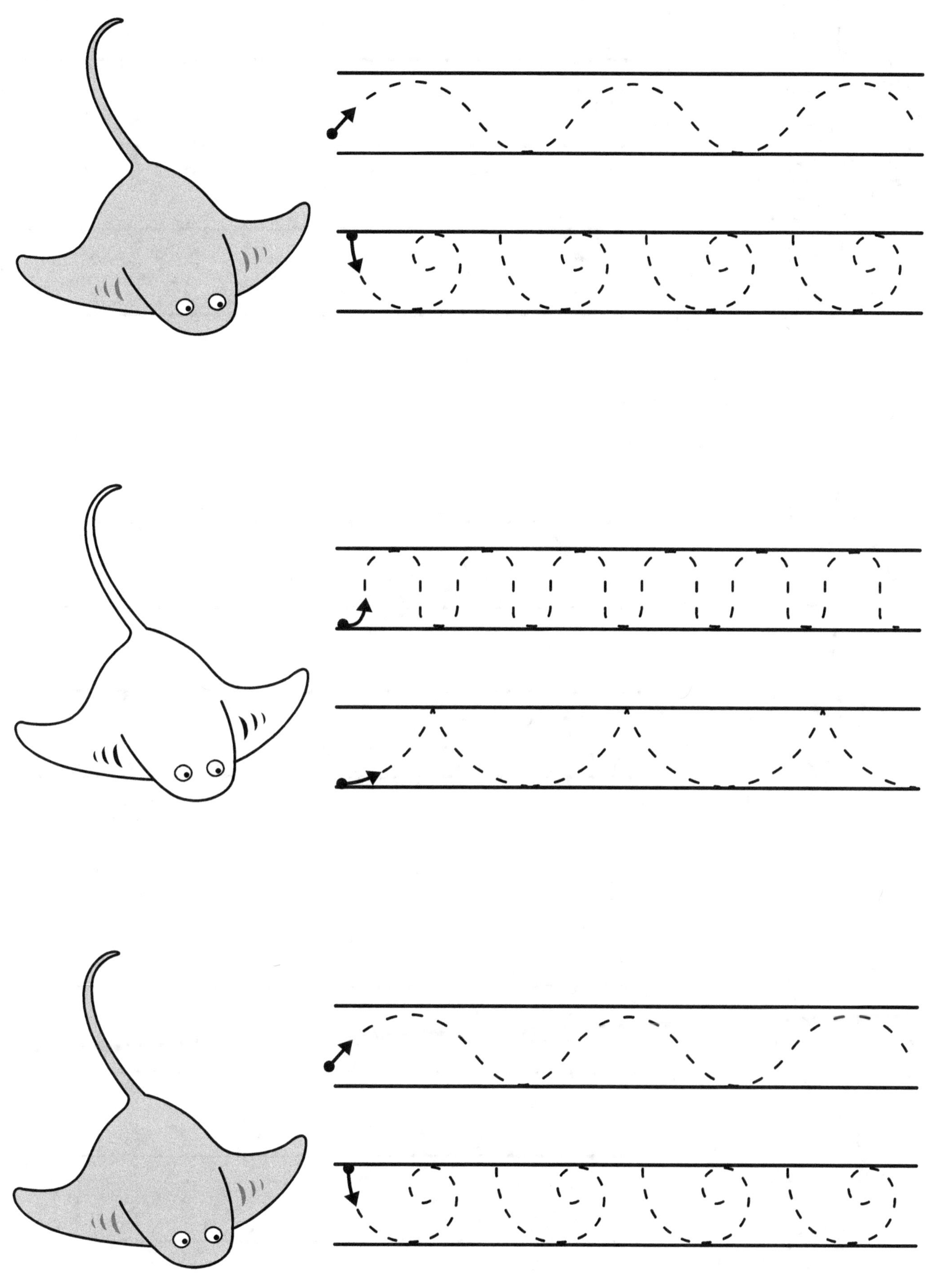

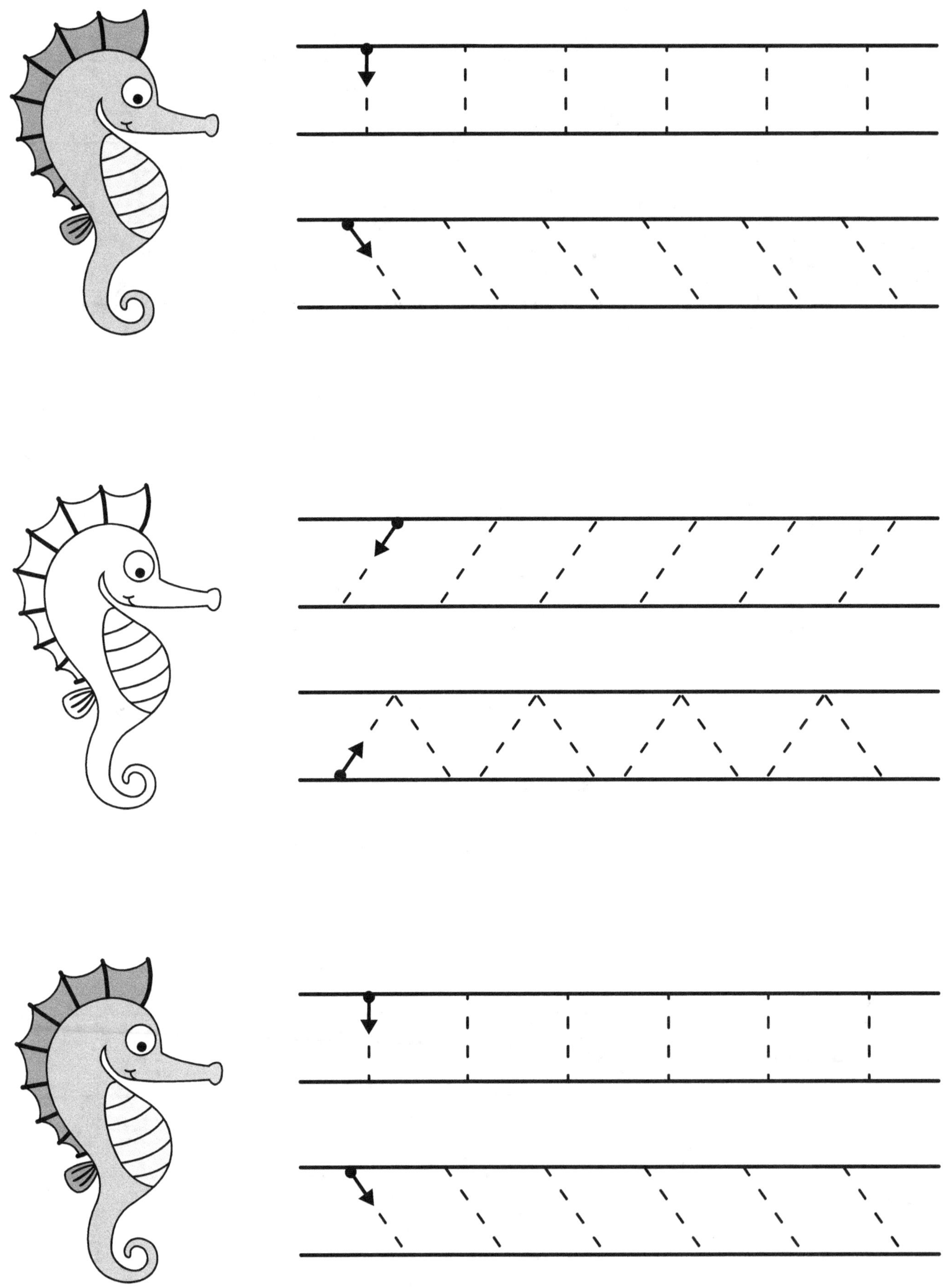

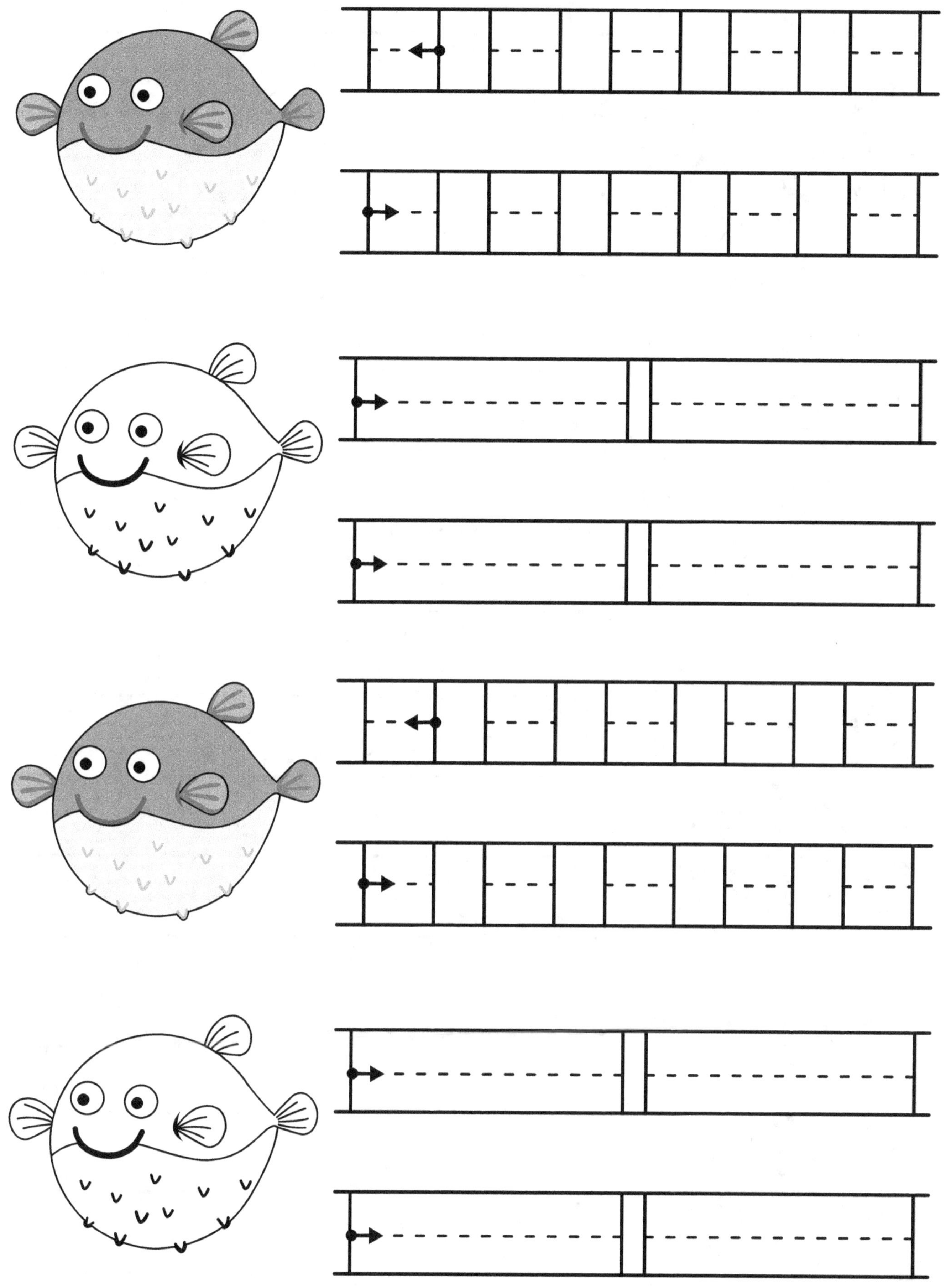

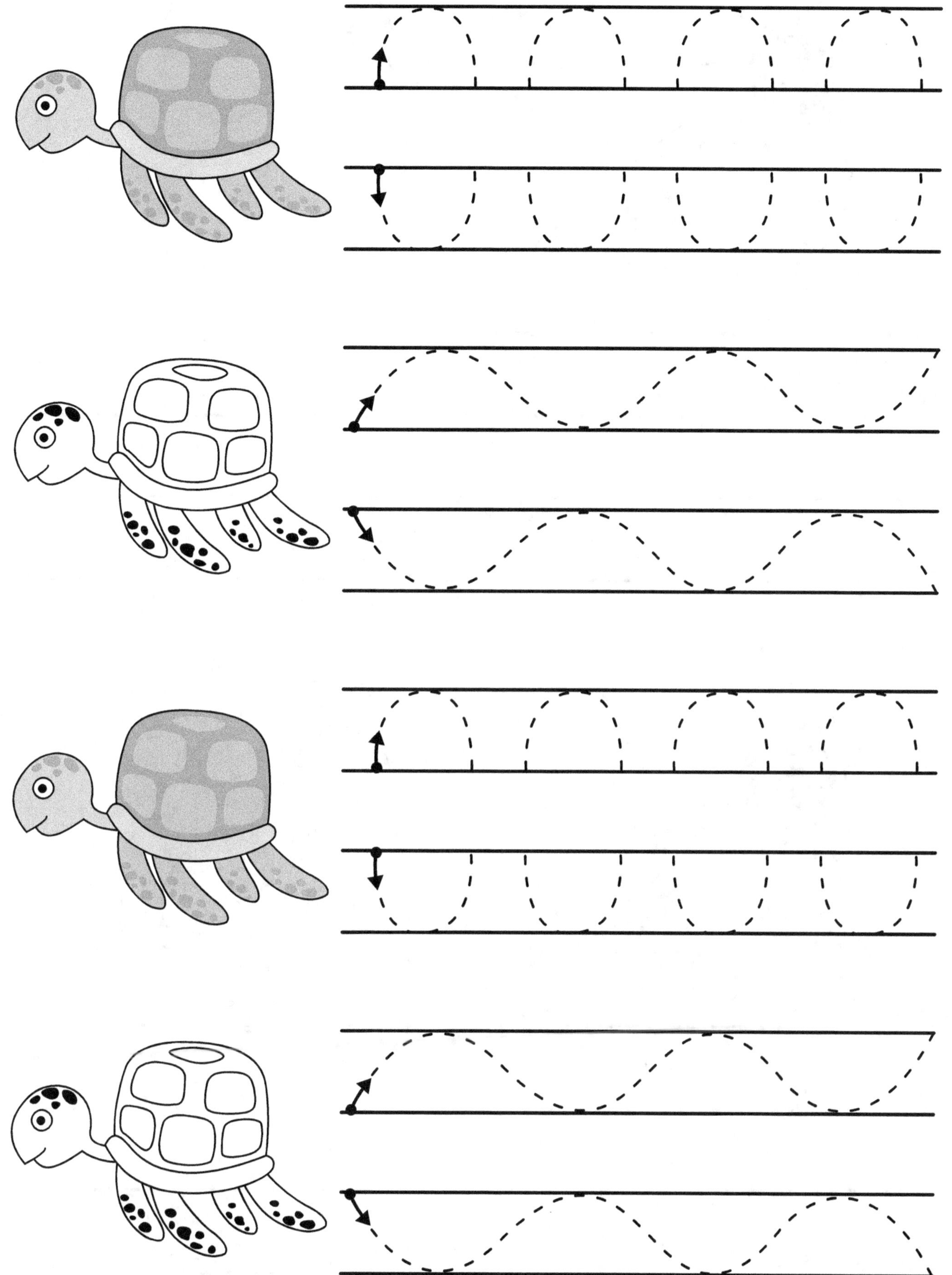

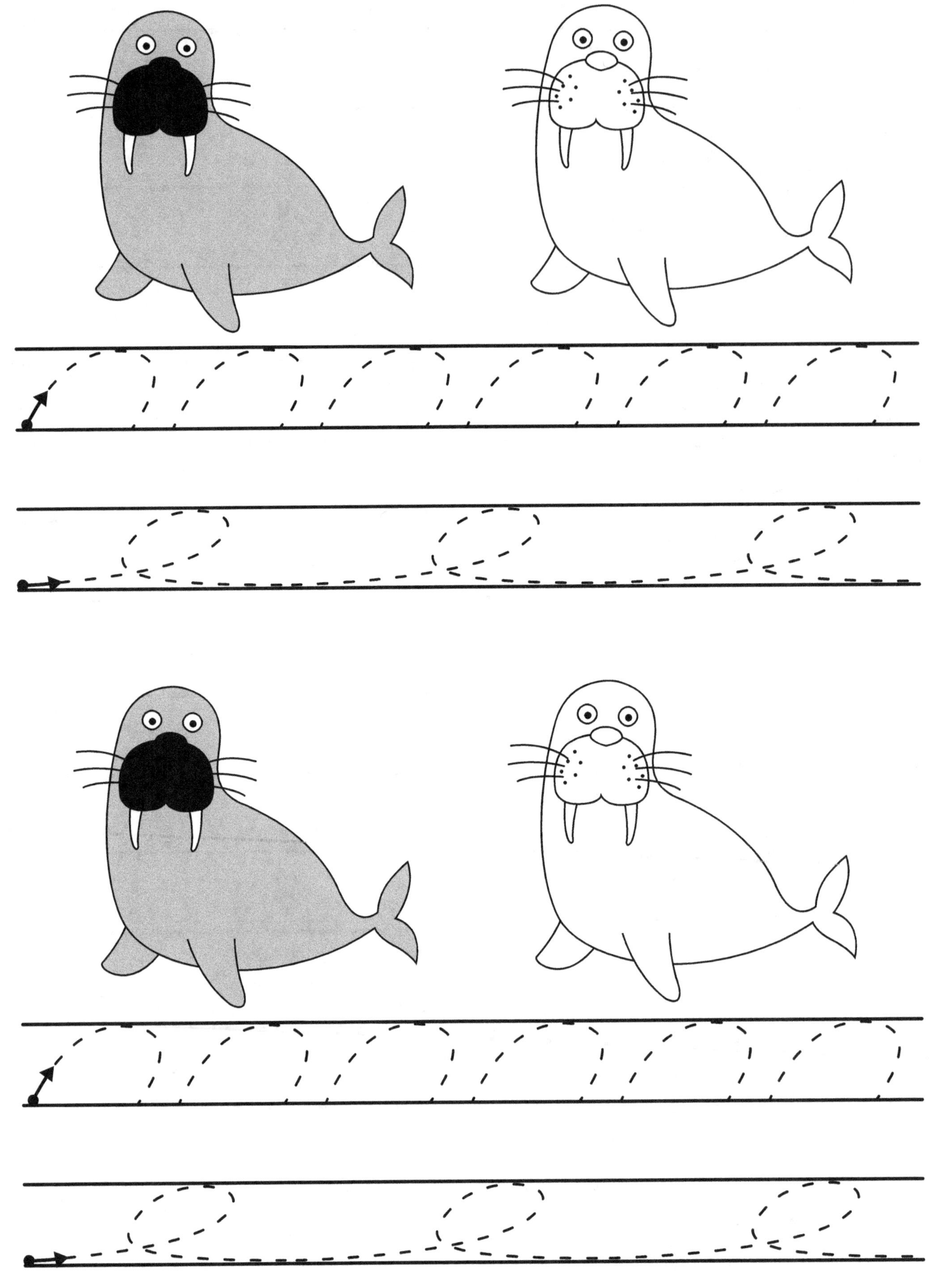

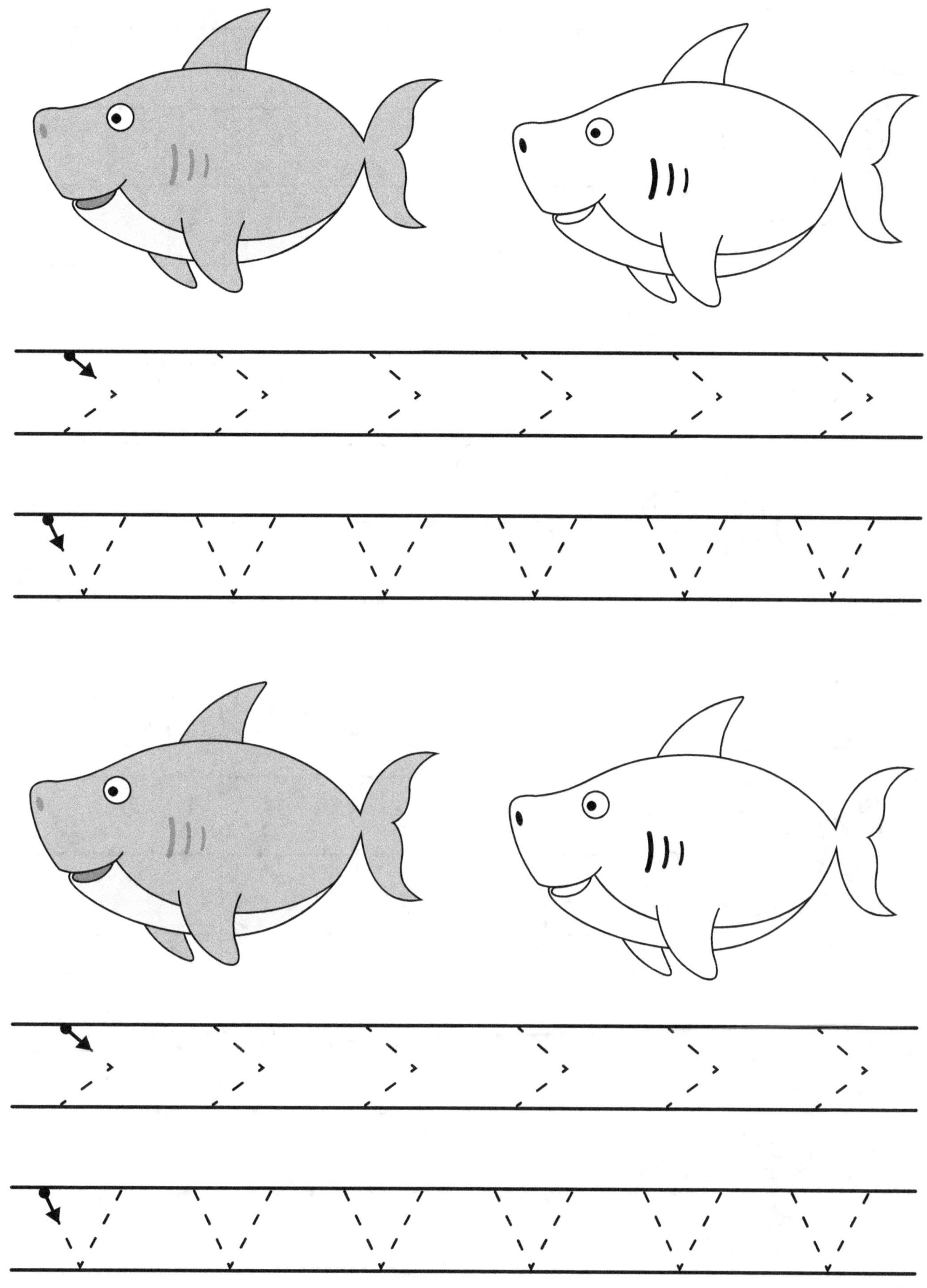

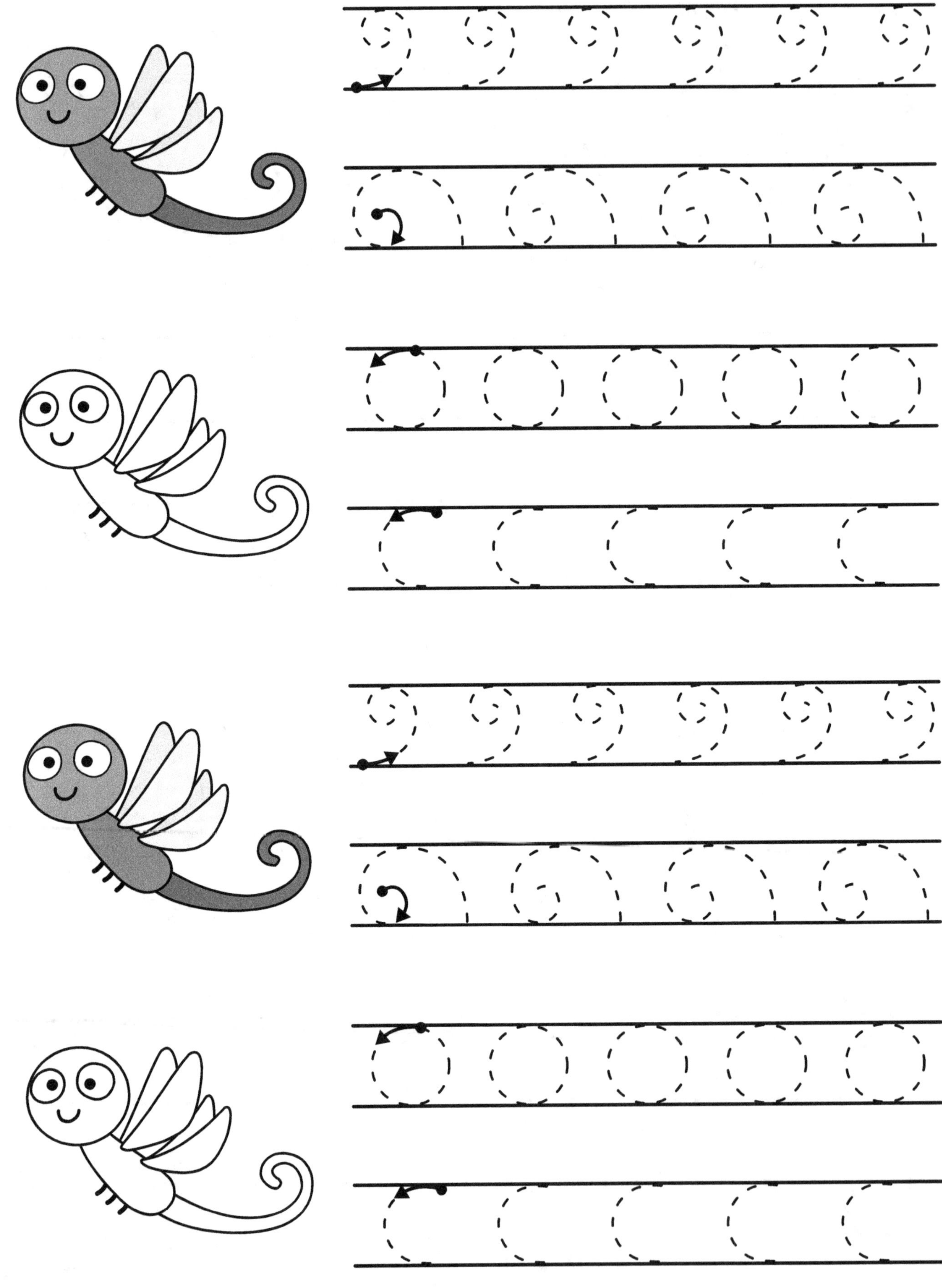

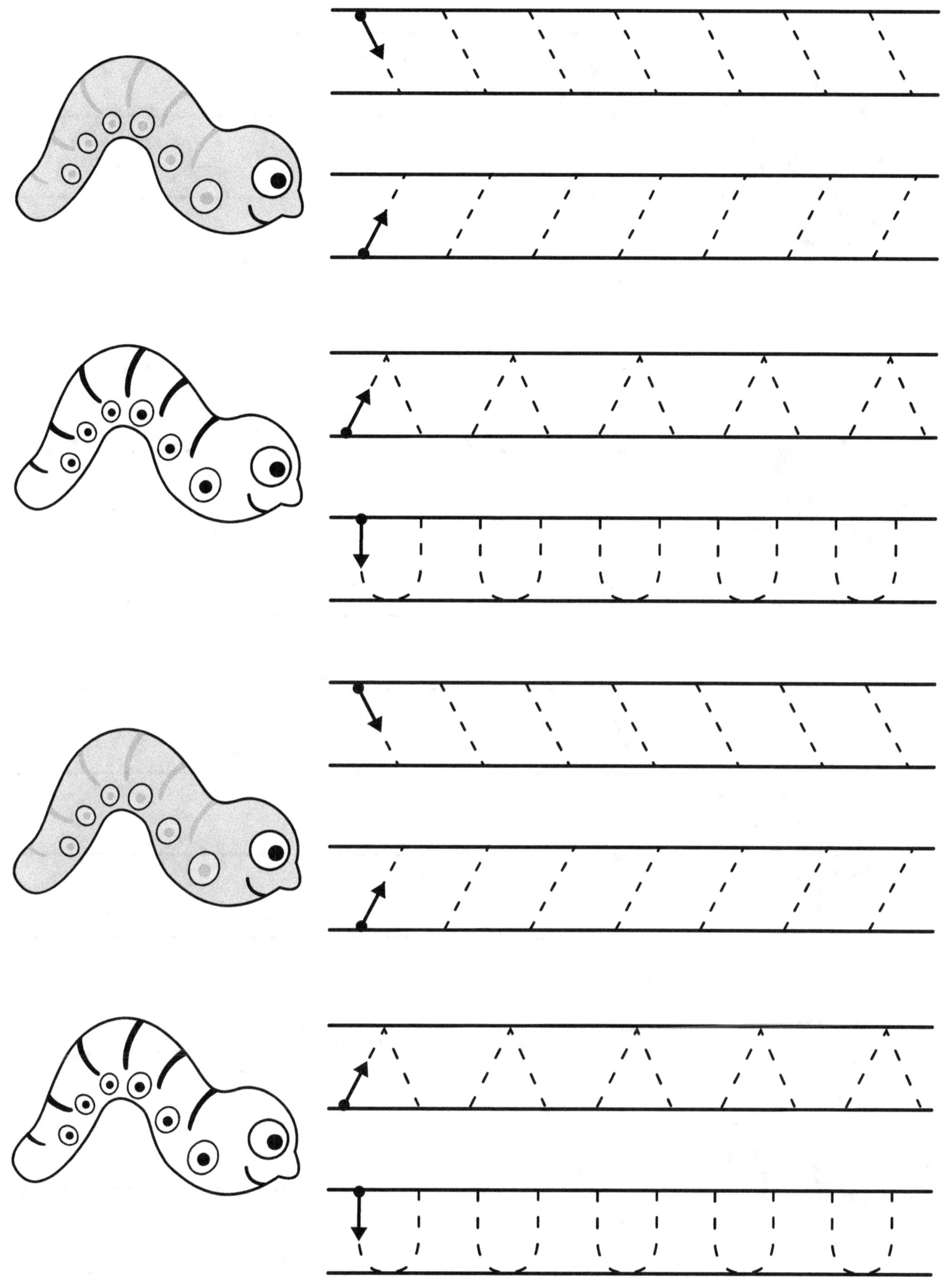

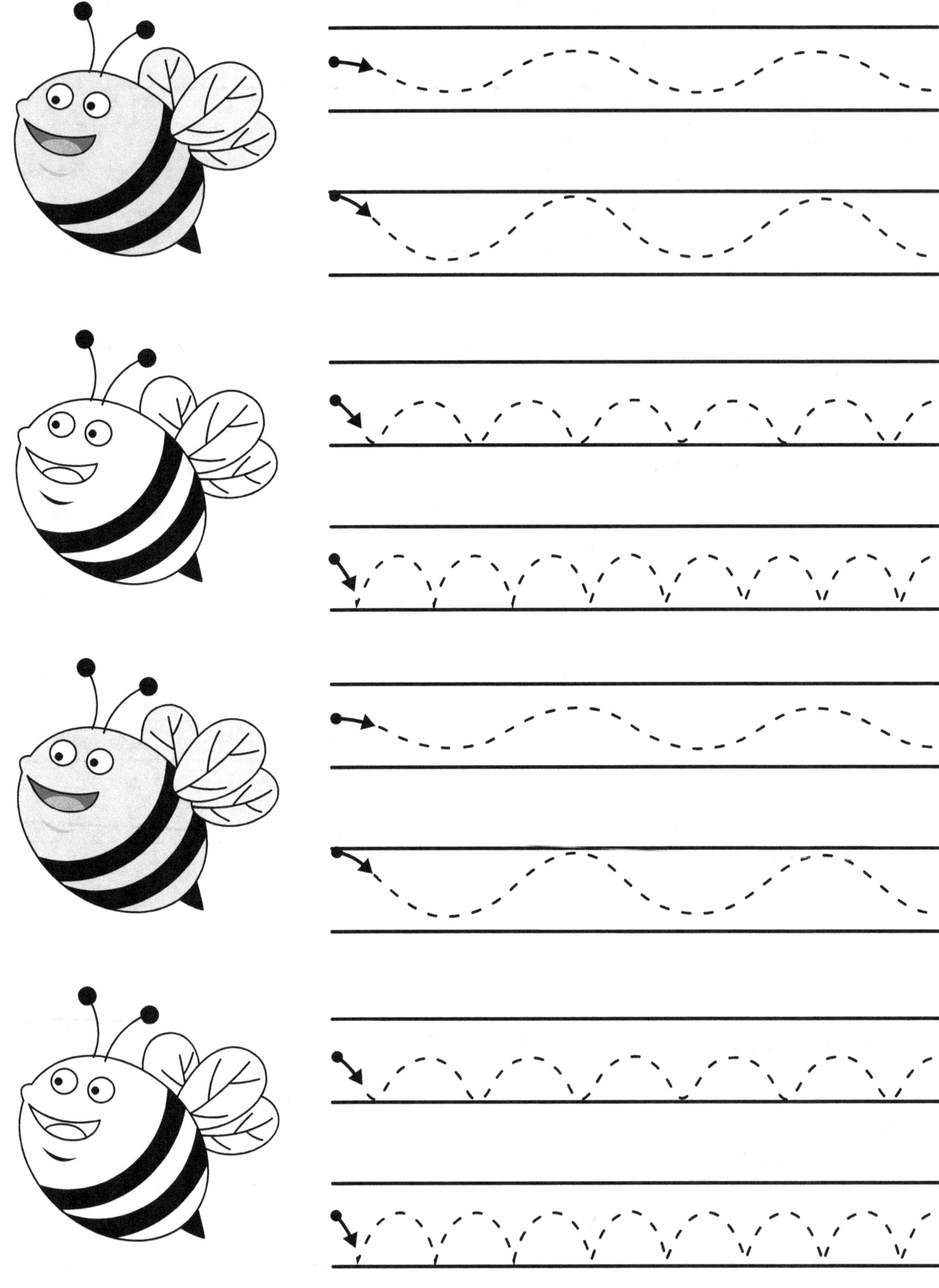

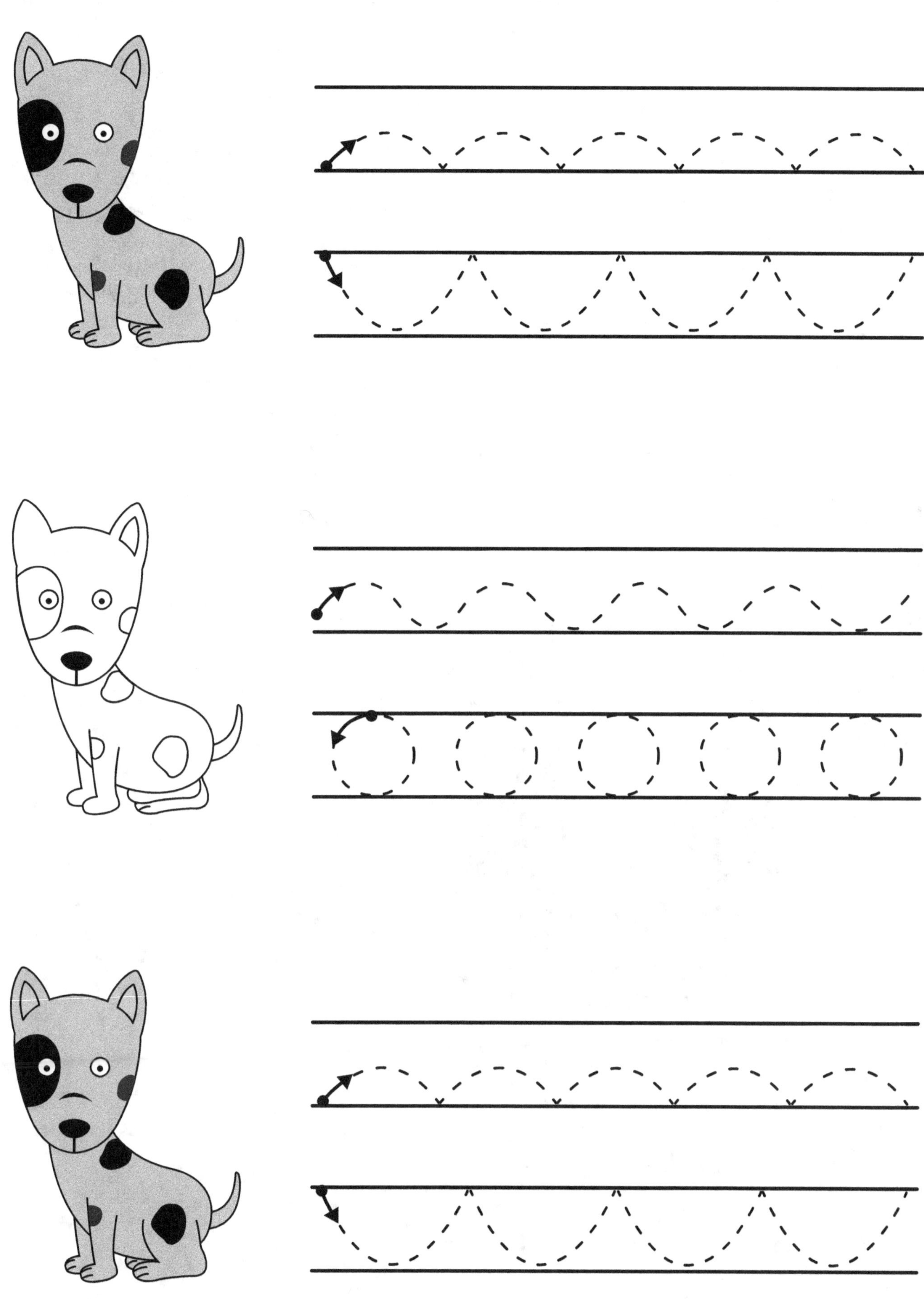

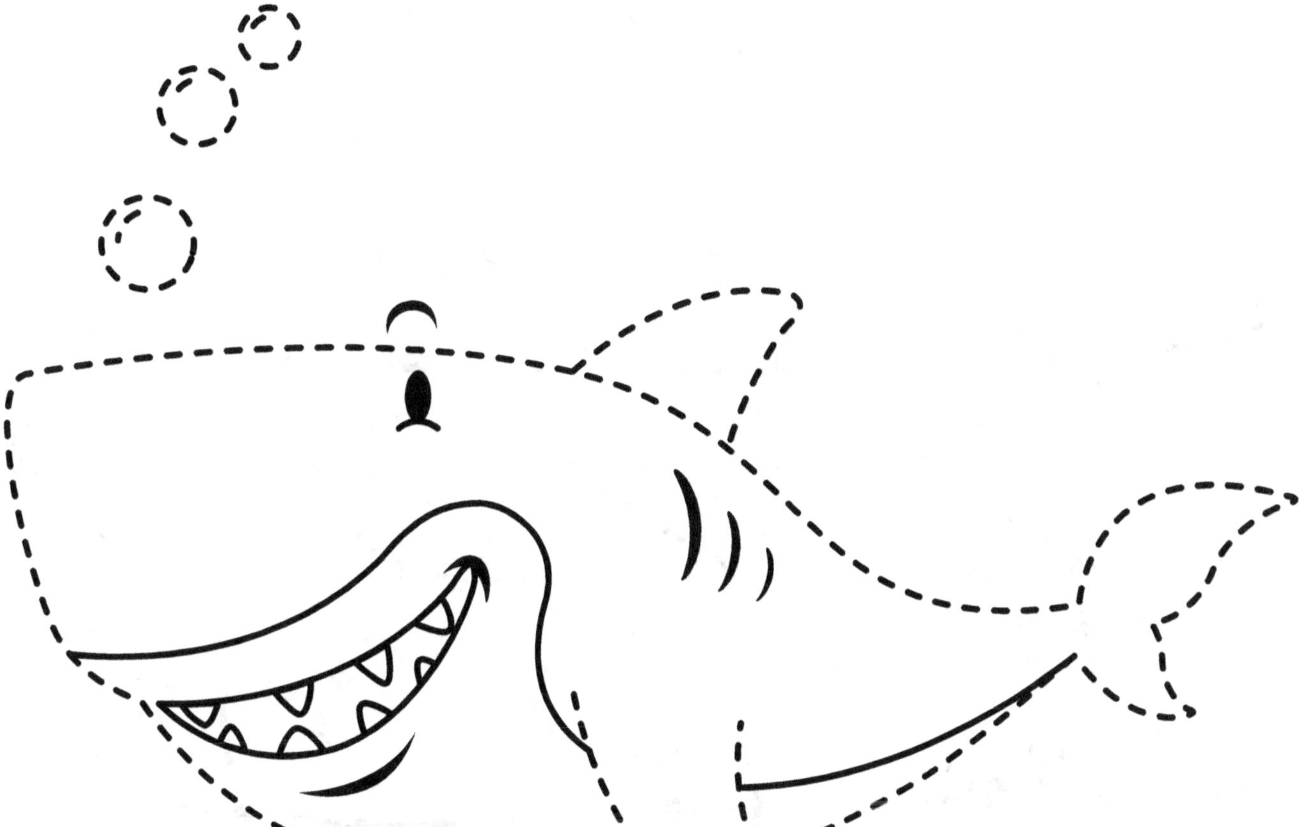

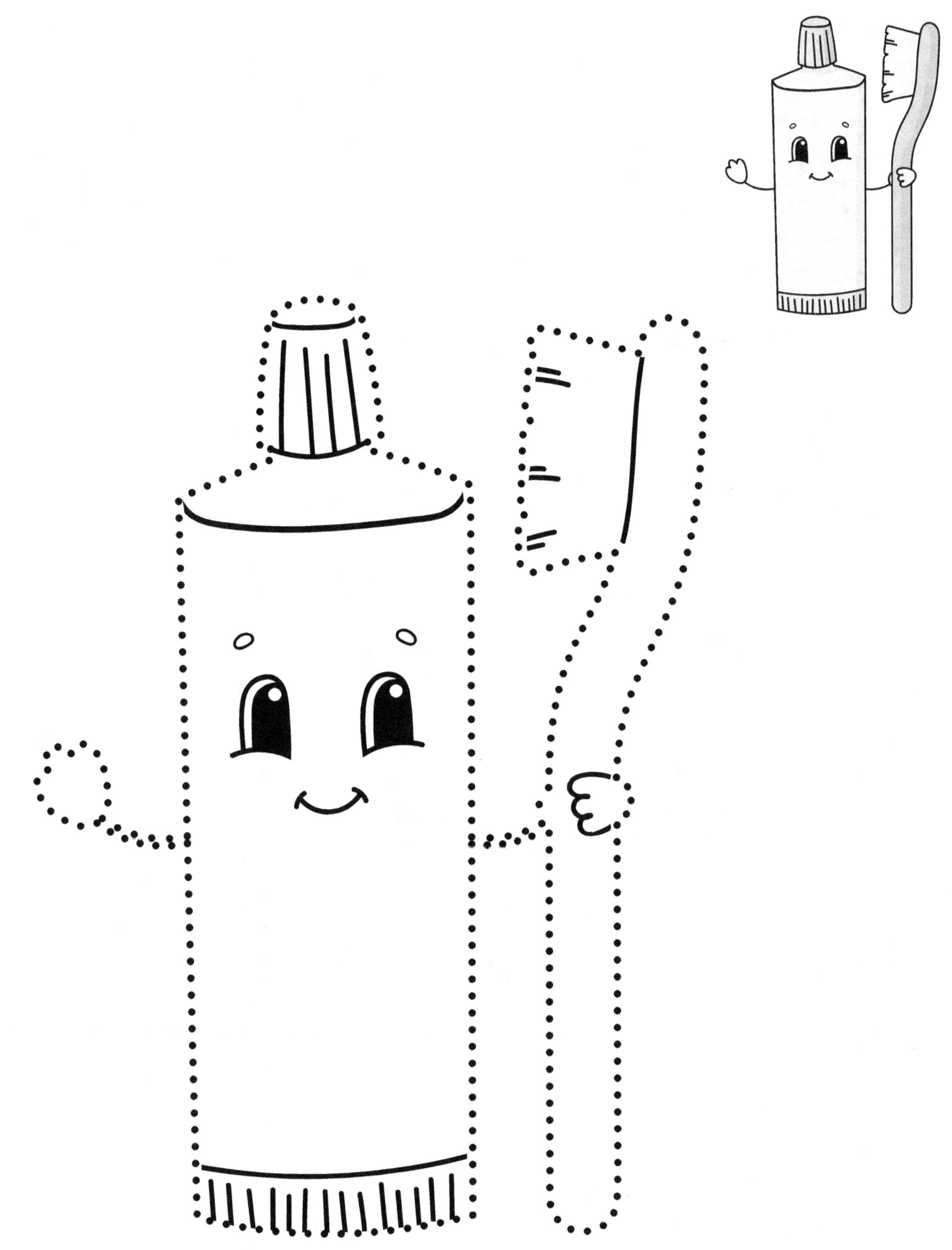

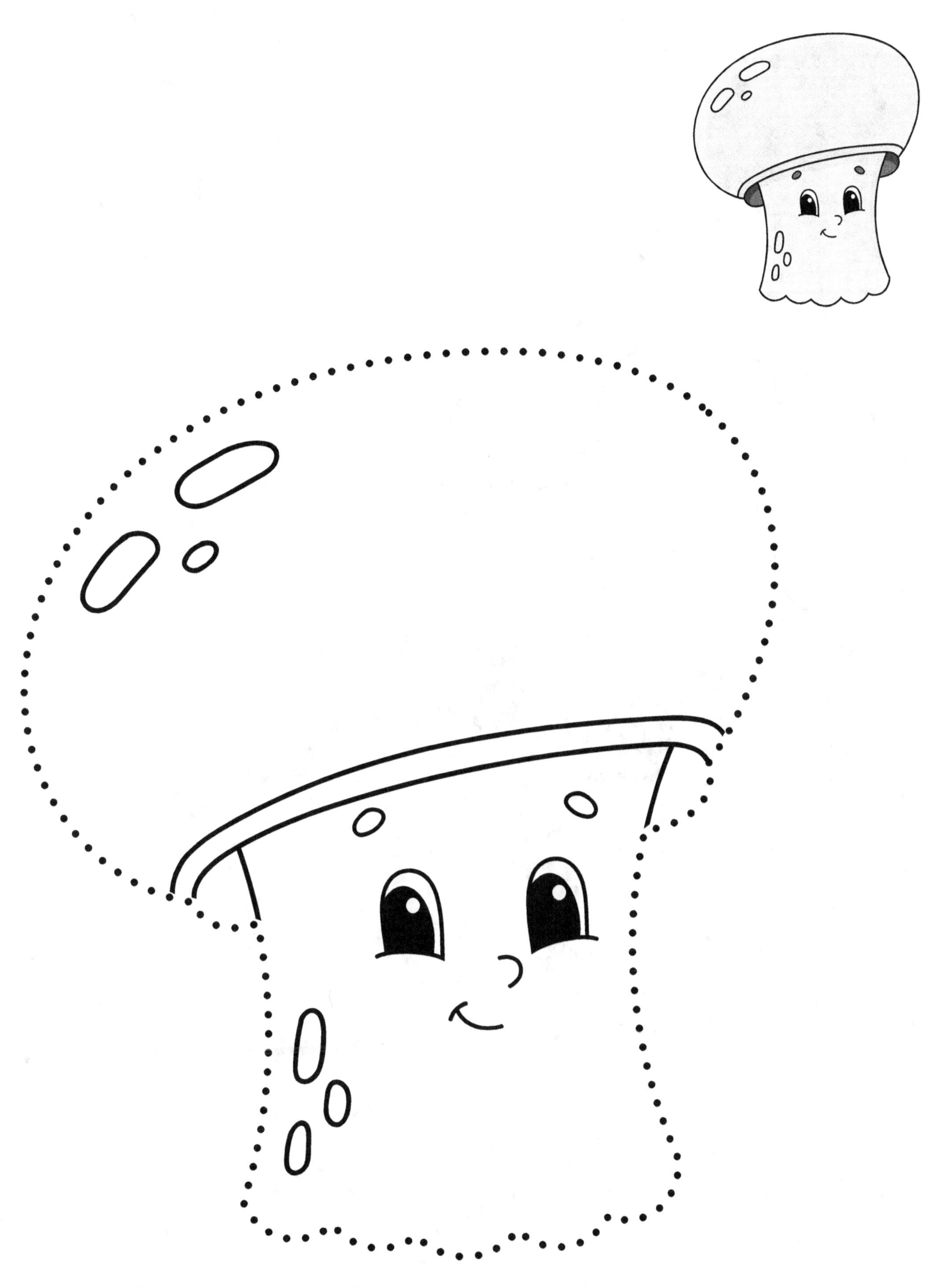

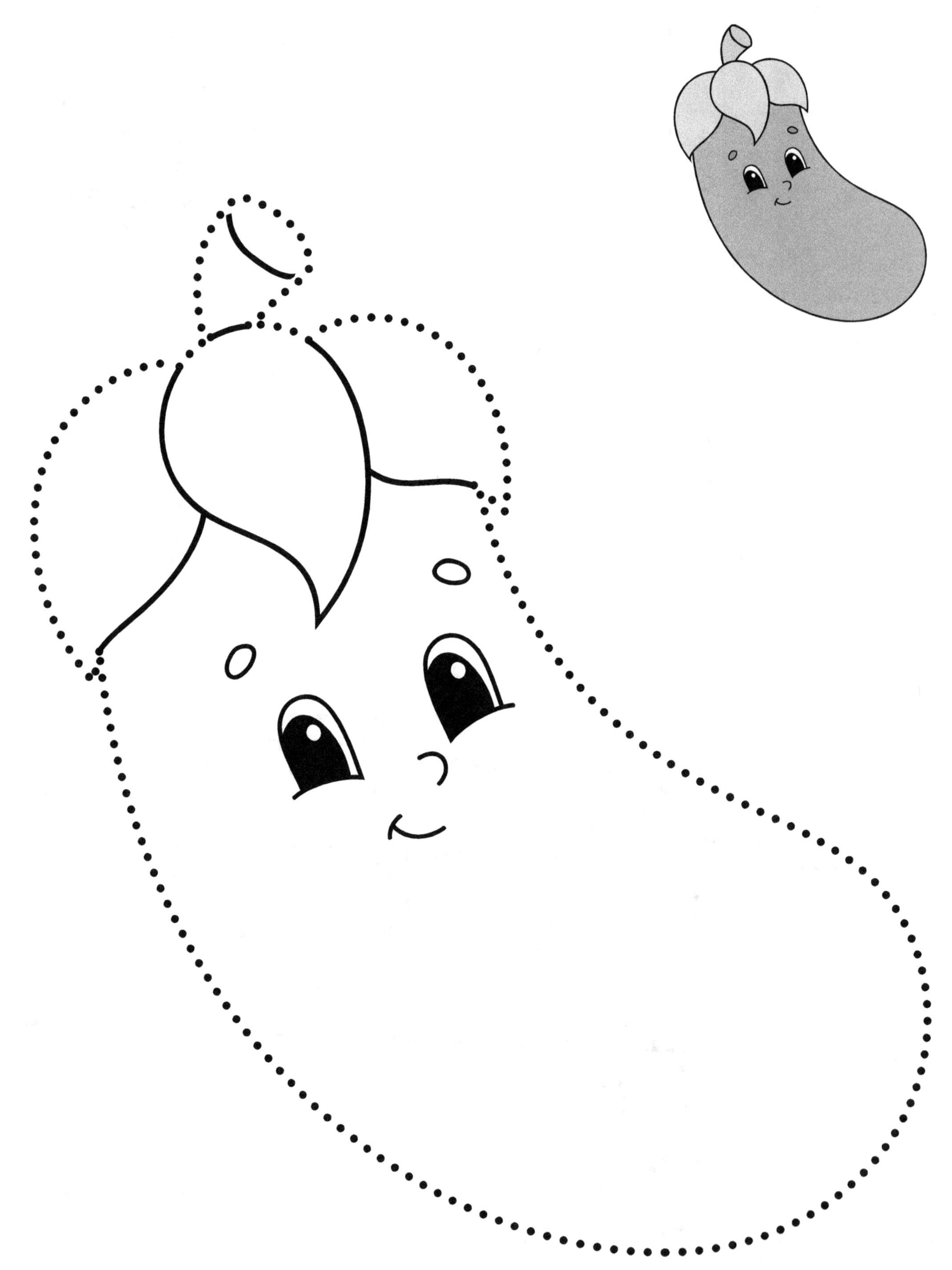

Lena Rakete

LENA

Mathias Buhl · Humplgassl 10 · 82515 Wolfratshausen · Germany

My Sight Word List

a	in	said
and	is	see
away	it	the
big	jump	three
blue	little	to
can	look	two
come	make	up
down	me	we
find	my	where
for	not	yellow
funny	one	you
go	day	
help	play	
here	red	
I	run	

Name: _______________ Date: _______________

Today is: Monday   Tuesday   Wednesday
Thursday   Friday

Direction: Trace and read the sentences.

fun	gun	run	sun
zabawa	pistolet	biegać	słońce

They are having fun.

He has a gun.

The bear is running.

The sun is smiling.